THE *Mighty* COLORADO RIVER

From the Glaciers to the Gulf

JIM TURNER

RIO NUEVO
PUBLISHERS

To Susan Bail Adams,
who listened patiently,
gave me confidence,
and kept me laughing.

Rio Nuevo Publishers®
P. O. Box 5250
Tucson, AZ 85703-0250
(520) 623-9558, www.rionuevo.com

COVER: The Colorado River carves Horseshoe Bend near Page, Arizona.
TITLE PAGE: The Grand Canyon drops straight down 3,000 feet (880 m) here at Toroweap,
offering a most striking view of the river.
CONTENTS PAGE: Toroweap, on the west end of the Grand Canyon. It is difficult to access,
but worth the trip.

Managing editor: Aaron Downey
Book design: David Jenney Design
Map: Patti Isaacs, 45th Parallel Maps and Infographics

Printed in Korea.

10   9   8   7   6   5   4   3   2

Library of Congress Cataloging-in-Publication Data

Names: Turner, Jim (James Edward), 1949– author.
Title: The mighty Colorado River : from the glaciers to the gulf / Jim Turner.
Description: Tucson, AZ : Rio Nuevo Publishers, 2016.
Identifiers: LCCN 2015048189 | ISBN 9781940322049 (pbk.) | ISBN 1940322049
  (pbk.)
Subjects: LCSH: Colorado River (Colo.-Mexico)—Pictorial works. | Colorado
  River Valley (Colo.-Mexico)—Pictorial works. | Natural history—Colorado
  River (Colo.-Mexico)—Pictorial works. | Natural history—Colorado River
  Valley (Colo.-Mexico)—Pictorial works.
Classification: LCC F788 .T87 2016 | DDC 979.1/3—dc23
LC record available at http://lccn.loc.gov/2015048189

Contents

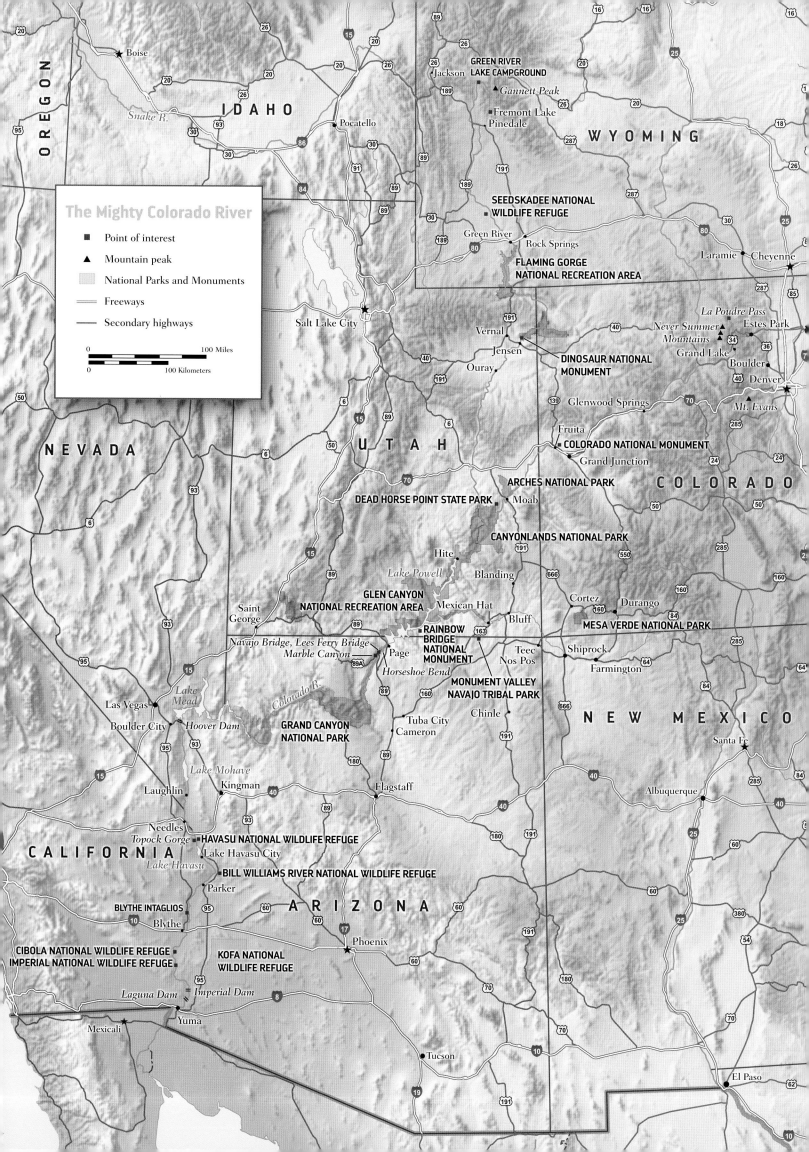

The Mighty Colorado River

- ■ Point of interest
- ▲ Mountain peak
- National Parks and Monuments
- ═══ Freeways
- ─── Secondary highways

0   100 Miles
0   100 Kilometers

OREGON

IDAHO

★ Boise

Snake R.

● Pocatello

WYOMING

★ Jackson

GREEN RIVER
LAKE CAMPGROUND

▲ *Gannett Peak*

■ *Fremont Lake*
Pinedale

SEEDSKADEE NATIONAL
■ WILDLIFE REFUGE

Green River ● Rock Springs

Laramie ● Cheyenne

FLAMING GORGE
NATIONAL RECREATION AREA

La Poudre Pass

★ Salt Lake City

Vernal

Jensen

Ouray

DINOSAUR NATIONAL
MONUMENT

*Never Summer
Mountains* ▲▲ Estes Park

Grand Lake ● Boulder

● Denver ★

Glenwood Springs

Mt. Evans ▲

Fruita ■ COLORADO NATIONAL MONUMENT

Grand Junction ●

UTAH

COLORADO

DEAD HORSE POINT STATE PARK

ARCHES NATIONAL PARK

● Moab

NEVADA

CANYONLANDS NATIONAL PARK

Hite ●

Lake Powell

Blanding ●

Saint
George

GLEN CANYON
NATIONAL RECREATION AREA

Mexican Hat ●

Bluff ●

Cortez ●

Durango ●

MESA VERDE NATIONAL PARK

RAINBOW
■ BRIDGE
NATIONAL
MONUMENT

Navajo Bridge, Lees Ferry Bridge
Marble Canyon ● Page

Teec
Nos Pos ●

Shiprock ●

Farmington ●

Horseshoe Bend

MONUMENT VALLEY
NAVAJO TRIBAL PARK

Las Vegas ●

Lake Mead

Colorado R.

Boulder City ●

Hoover Dam

GRAND CANYON
NATIONAL PARK

Tuba City ●
Cameron ●

Chinle ●

NEW MEXICO

Santa Fe ★

Lake Mohave

Laughlin ●

Kingman ●

Flagstaff ●

Albuquerque ●

Needles ●

Topock Gorge

■ HAVASU NATIONAL WILDLIFE REFUGE

Lake Havasu City ●

Lake Havasu

BILL WILLIAMS RIVER NATIONAL WILDLIFE REFUGE

Parker ●

CALIFORNIA

ARIZONA

BLYTHE INTAGLIOS

● Blythe

Phoenix ★

CIBOLA NATIONAL WILDLIFE REFUGE ■
IMPERIAL NATIONAL WILDLIFE REFUGE ■

KOFA NATIONAL
WILDLIFE REFUGE

Laguna Dam ═ *Imperial Dam*

● Yuma

Mexicali ●

Tucson ●

El Paso ●

Introduction

THE COLORADO RIVER BASIN, combining the flows of the Colorado and Green rivers, is one of the most magnificent collections of natural wonders in the world. The river is 1,400 miles long, the second longest in the United States, and its drainage basin covers 244,000 square miles, a twelfth of the nation. That is an area greater than Spain and Portugal combined.

The Colorado River Basin drains more than fifty rivers and streams in seven western states: Wyoming, Colorado, Utah, New Mexico, Arizona, Nevada, and California. The river travels through the driest terrain in the nation. It goes through hundreds of miles of deep canyons, exposing rock formations more than a billion years old. Deep canyons, rugged mountains, and great deserts make the basin one of the most sparsely settled areas in North America. The area contains almost every extreme of precipitation, geological formation, altitude, and temperature, and the two rivers travel through more natural scenic areas than any other water source in the country. Following the Green and Colorado rivers, one encounters dozens of national parks, national monuments, wildlife refuges, and national recreation areas.

Like the Colorado River, the text in this book flows downstream, making unexpected turns, winding up in unusual eddies, and sometimes shifting abruptly from one background to another. When you follow a river, you have to adapt quickly, especially when packing the whole journey into a very short time. Like the kayakers and rafters, the writer would like to take his time, but the river doesn't always let him. The river sets its own pace, chooses rapid changes in scenery and elevation, and ultimately decides how the story will end.

Every community along the banks has its own flavor and character, but because of climate and geography, they often share more similarities than differences. By natural law, rivers start in the mountains, flow down to the prairies, then into canyons, gaining power and size as other rivers join them, until they reach the ocean.

The beauty of the Colorado River Basin is how much land has been set aside, not only for visitors to enjoy and appreciate, but to preserve nature's wonders. Down the rivers from Flaming Gorge National Recreation Area and Rocky Mountain National Park to Dinosaur National

Monument, Colorado National Monument, Arches National Park,
Canyonlands National Park, then on down to Glen Canyon National
Recreation Area, Grand Canyon National Park, Lake Mead National
Recreation Area, Havasu, Bill Williams, and Kofa wilderness areas, one
could travel these river sites all year long from summer in the mountains
to winter in the deserts and never tire of visiting these national treasures.

From prehistoric times, there is one basic truth: where there is water,
there will be plants and animals—including humans. River towns con-
nect the people to nature and give them a commonality. At their sources,
both the Green and Colorado river areas are great for skiing, hunting,
and fishing. Towns like Pinedale, Wyoming, and Vail, Colorado, are
prime examples of high mountain river towns.

As the rivers flow to flat prairies, farm towns like Vernal, Utah, Glenwood Springs, Colorado, and Green River, Utah, support the mountain
towns. Farther down, as the Green and Colorado cut deep canyons into
the Tavaputs and Colorado plateaus, desert towns like Moab, Utah, and
Las Vegas, Nevada, now serve boating, camping, and another kind of
skiing (on water this time). And most of all, there are those who come to
marvel at nature's majestic landscapes.

OPPOSITE~This battered metal boat, built
by Bert Loper and named the "Ross
Wheeler," was left high and dry on the
rocks in the Grand Canyon after a film-
ing expedition on Slate Creek in 1915. It
was dragged there by John Waltenberg
and the National Park Service has been
caring for it ever since.

BELOW~Strange but true, this is an
unaltered photograph of the confluence of the Green and Colorado rivers.
The Green, above, gets very little runoff,
while the red silt in the Colorado comes
from flash flooding in creeks above
Moab, Utah, with names like Bloody
Mary Wash that turn the river bright red
or even neon orange.

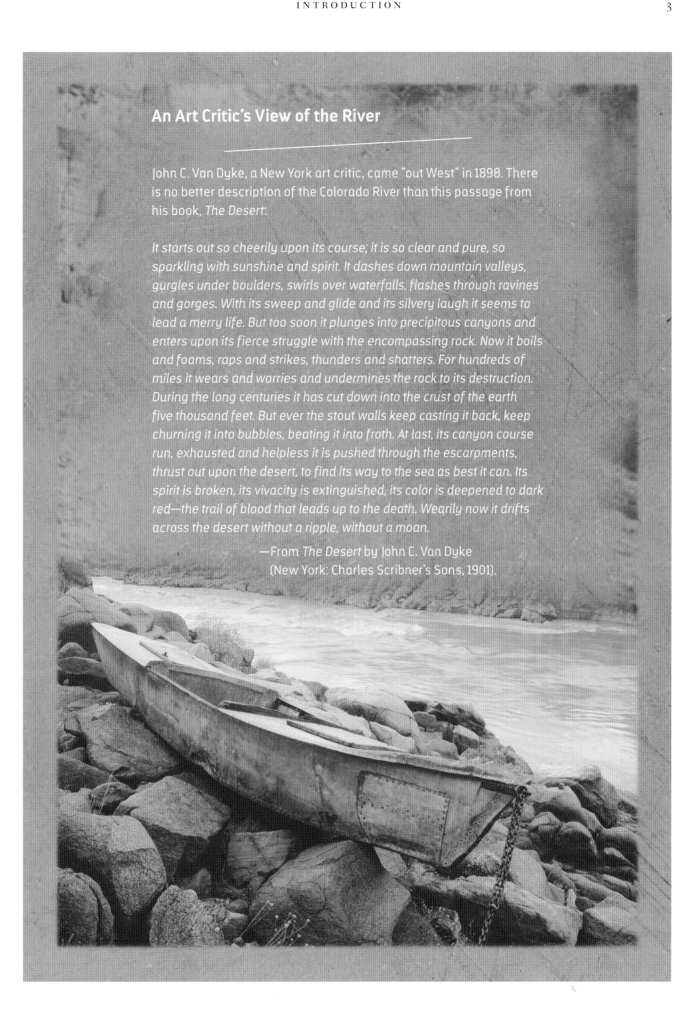

An Art Critic's View of the River

John C. Van Dyke, a New York art critic, came "out West" in 1898. There is no better description of the Colorado River than this passage from his book, *The Desert*:

It starts out so cheerily upon its course; it is so clear and pure, so sparkling with sunshine and spirit. It dashes down mountain valleys, gurgles under boulders, swirls over waterfalls, flashes through ravines and gorges. With its sweep and glide and its silvery laugh it seems to lead a merry life. But too soon it plunges into precipitous canyons and enters upon its fierce struggle with the encompassing rock. Now it boils and foams, raps and strikes, thunders and shatters. For hundreds of miles it wears and worries and undermines the rock to its destruction. During the long centuries it has cut down into the crust of the earth five thousand feet. But ever the stout walls keep casting it back, keep churning it into bubbles, beating it into froth. At last, its canyon course run, exhausted and helpless it is pushed through the escarpments, thrust out upon the desert, to find its way to the sea as best it can. Its spirit is broken, its vivacity is extinguished, its color is deepened to dark red—the trail of blood that leads up to the death. Wearily now it drifts across the desert without a ripple, without a moan.

—From *The Desert* by John C. Van Dyke
(New York: Charles Scribner's Sons, 1901).

Chapter 1

The Green River

A River Named for Its Color

The Shoshone Indians call it Seeds-kee-dee-Agie, for the prairie hens (sage grouse) plentiful in its upper basin. Spanish explorers called it the Rio Verde, or Green River, probably because of the lush plant life along the banks.

It starts in the Wind River Range, known to local folks as "The Winds." They are a part of the Rocky Mountain chain, and the Continental Divide, the dividing line where waters flow either west to the Pacific Ocean or east to the Gulf of Mexico. The divide runs along the crest of these mountains. The range includes Gannett Peak, the highest peak in Wyoming at 13,804 feet (4,207 m). Nineteen more peaks in the Winds top 13,000 feet (3,962 m). Twenty-seven glaciers on the western slopes of the Winds formed many lakes there over millions of years. Gannett Glacier, twenty miles northwest of Green River Lakes, is the largest single glacier in the U.S. Rocky Mountains. The runoff from this glacier is a main source for the Green River. The melting glaciers stream down the granite mountain slopes to Green River Lakes, elevation 8,040 feet (2,451 m). From those icy trickles, the Green River begins.

OPPOSITE~Fremont Peak and others tower above Island Lake in the Wind River Range, Bridger-Teton National Forest.

RIGHT~Icy blue glacier waters tumble through Titcomb Basin, twenty miles southeast of the Green River's source.

From there, the river widens and meanders through meadows and ranchlands. You can see fishermen standing in small flat skiffs on wider, slower stretches of the river. Fifty miles southwest of the lake, the town of Pinedale serves residents, sportsmen, and tourists.

Pinedale, Wyoming

Surrounded by three mountain ranges—the Wyoming, Wind River, and Gros Ventre—Pinedale is the heart of the Upper Green River Valley. With a population just over two thousand, Pinedale residents describe themselves as "a relaxed, rural community, which serves as a recreational gateway to the Wind River Mountains and Bridger Wilderness area."

Although not on the banks of the Green River, it is a river town. Every river town has its own character, and this one is a combination mountain village, outdoor sports depot, and free spirit haven. At an elevation of 7,100 feet (2,164 m), the town's "Altitude Pharmacy" describes its alpine setting. Wildlife in this area includes elk, moose, deer, and large populations of pronghorn.

The Pronghorn Is Not an Antelope

Although it resembles the true Old World antelopes, pronghorns are a unique North American mammal that originated in the Pleistocene epoch (2.5 million to 11,700 years ago). For almost 7,000 years, the largest pronghorn herd on Earth has migrated 150 miles (one of the world's longest land-animal migrations) from their summer range in the Grand

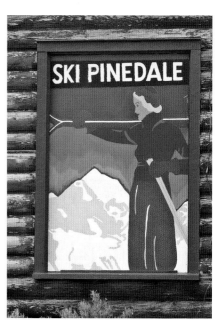

Poster on the side of one of several sports outfitters in Pinedale, Wyoming. It's on Pine Street, which is also Highway 191, just a few blocks from Pine Creek.

TOP~Fly fishing on the Green River in the Wind River Mountains about thirty miles from the river's source.

Tetons to the Pinedale area for its warmth, water, and forage.

Unlike most other horned animals, both male and female pronghorns have backward-curving horns. These are not bone antlers like deer and elk; pronghorns' horns are made of a blade of bone covered with a keratinous material similar to human fingernails, which they shed annually. The horns do not branch, but have one forward-pointing prong that gives them their name. Bison, bighorn sheep, and cattle also have keratinous horns. Second only to the cheetah for the title of fastest land animal, the pronghorn can reach speeds of 55 mph. In the spring, females give birth to one or two calves, which are able to outrun a human in just a few days.

LEFT~This is pronghorn country. They are elusive and unmatched for their beauty, grace, and speed.

BELOW~Sunrise along the banks of the Green River in Wyoming.

Green River Mountain Men

The rendezvous was a fantasy, a saturnalia. Everything swam in a cedar-red haze of raw corn liquor and thousands of campfires and the Indians dancing around them all night, the incessant racing of the horses against spotted Indian ponies, the gambling games carried out wherever a blanket could be thrown.

—FRANK WATERS, *The Colorado*, 1946

When Beau Brummel first appeared in a stove-pipe beaver-felt hat in 1799, the American fur industry exploded overnight, opening the western frontier from the Mississippi River to the Pacific Ocean. Everyone had to have a hat like his, and that took a lot of beaver pelts. Forty years later, fashions changed and the market collapsed, but because of the fur trappers' hunt for beaver, the great majority of the West had been explored.

Capitalizing on the fur trade, William Henry Ashley, land speculator, gunpowder manufacturer, and Missouri politician, joined with bullet maker Andrew Henry to form the Rocky Mountain Fur Company. In 1822, they advertised for one hundred men to go fur trapping. Some recruits became American legends: Jim Bridger, Kit Carson, Jedediah Smith, and emancipated slave James Beckwourth.

The Green River Valley near the present-day towns of Pinedale and Daniel was the center of the Rocky Mountain fur trade, and six major spring and summer rendezvous were held in that area. As many as three thousand trappers and Indians came from hundreds of miles to attend these trade fairs.

Celebrating the Mountain Men

Pinedale, Wyoming, is famous for its two-story Museum of the Mountain Man, reminiscent of a giant hunting lodge. The museum exhibits rare artifacts, such as Jim Bridger's rifle and fur trade documents from the early 1800s. Since 1935, Pinedale has also hosted the Green River Rendezvous Pageant. Main attractions include a Northern Arapaho Native American Dance, a three-on-three basketball tournament, and a kids' fishing derby.

Eleven miles west and two miles south of Pinedale is Daniel, Wyoming, population 150, former location of the Green River Rendezvous. The area was declared a National Historic Landmark in 1961. Of the sixteen rendezvous held in Wyoming between 1824 and 1840, six were located near Daniel.

Seedskadee National Wildlife Refuge

North of Green River, Wyoming, Seedskadee National Wildlife Refuge borders thirty-six miles along the Green River. Here, the river is an oasis that bisects southwest Wyoming's sagebrush plains and high desert. Seedskadee National Wildlife Refuge was established in 1965 to offset the loss of natural habitat from the construction of the Fontenelle Reservoir on the Green River. The refuge's 27,230 acres include river, riparian, wetland, and sagebrush habitats. This vital, lush river corridor is home to more than 250 species of resident and migrant wildlife. In the right season, you may spot trumpeter swans, pronghorn, moose, coyotes, and bald eagles. The Seedskadee National Wildlife Refuge is a popular area for bird watchers.

Introduced into the Seedskadee National Wildlife Refuge in the 1990s, the trumpeter swan population reached a record 303 in February of 2014, and they continue to thrive there.

Nomadic Indian tribes, fur trappers, and eventually early pioneers took advantage of this relatively flat area, and thousands of pioneers crossed the perilous Green River here. The Oregon and Mormon trails crossed here, and Jim Bridger and others operated ferries. The wagon ruts of the pioneer trails can still be seen in some parts of the Seedskadee National Wildlife Refuge.

Green River, Wyoming

About 120 miles south of Pinedale and 46 miles north of the Wyoming/Utah border, the Green River winds through the town of Green River, Wyoming. A natural pathway to the West, it incorporated in 1868 in what was then the Dakota Territory. The town was a division point for the Union Pacific Railroad, and it is still an important railroad town. Interstate 80 parallels both the river and the railroad tracks through the town, and the city is also surrounded by tall ridges of ancient sedimentary deposits. Soda ash is mined here from veins up to 1,600 feet (490 m) deep.

John Wesley Powell started both of his famous exploring expeditions of the Green River, the Colorado River, and the Grand Canyon from this town in 1869 and 1871. The town was the last place they knew of where they could launch their boats before the river was swallowed up by deep canyons and rushing rapids.

Ahead of the expedition were the picturesque Uinta Mountains (pronounced you-IN-tah) and the first of a series of magnificent canyons. Two days later Powell's expedition reached Flaming Gorge.

Flaming Gorge

In 1869, John Wesley Powell and his exploring party reached a spot on the Green River where bright sunlight radiated against brilliant red-orange cliffs, prompting them to name the place Flaming Gorge. The deep-red cliffs of Flaming Gorge were formed when the Uinta Mountains rose up 70 million years ago, while the Green River stayed in place and cut deep canyons through the ancient rocks.

In this area, John Wesley Powell's party floated in the relative calm of the river and saw an inscription cut into the canyon wall by fur trapper William Ashley that read simply, "Ashley 1825." The Flaming Gorge Reservoir was created when the dam was constructed in the canyon there in 1964. It rises 455 feet (140 m) above the river channel, and extends below the river bottom for another 47 feet (14 m), where it is anchored in bedrock. One million cubic yards (765,000 cm) of concrete were used to build the dam and power plant.

Managed by the USDA Forest Service as part of the Ashley National Forest, the Flaming Gorge National Recreation Area has more than six hundred camping and picnic sites around the ninety-one-mile-long reservoir. In addition to boating and rafting, there are more than two hundred miles of maintained trails for hiking and biking.

Major John Wesley Powell and Tau-Gu, a Kaibab Paiute leader, near Kanab, Utah, circa 1873.

When it comes to fishing, the upper Green River from its source to the tailwaters below the Flaming Gorge Reservoir is among the best in the West, an angler's dream. And for many local residents, hosting and guiding fishermen is a major part of their livelihoods. Flaming Gorge Reservoir is the high point of the area, where Mackinaw lake trout reach astounding weights of more than fifty pounds!

In addition, rainbow trout, smallmouth bass, and delicious Kokanee salmon are caught here. The waters below the Flaming Gorge Dam are regarded as a prime fly-fishing spot with abundant populations of huge rainbow, brown, and cutthroat trout. If it weren't for hunters and fisher-

men, hundreds of expedition companies and sporting goods stores in dozens of towns in Wyoming, Colorado, and northern Utah, as well as all the related businesses, like motels and boat rentals, cafés, markets, and gas stations, would have to close their doors. As one brochure says about the high country lakes and streams in the area, "fishing is fast and furious!"

ABOVE~The Green River winding through Flaming Gorge at sunset, clear and placid near the reservoir.

RIGHT~Clear, cold water makes for great fly fishing on the Green River.

Gates of Lodore

The Hole was a famous rendezvous of the trappers in old times. About here the hills stand off, terraced, of smooth-faced, burnt red sandstone, having the flats of the terraces clothed with the dark green of cedar and pine....Otter and ocelot and beaver lurked here, and the whole land is alive with the glitter of salient peaks, silver-tipped with snow. Even through the duskiest cañons goes the blue dart of the kingfisher, and the song of the water-ouzel rising like bubbles in a clear spring, and the crystal trickle of notes from the cañon wren.
— MARY AUSTIN, *The Land of Journey's Ending,* 1924

About twenty-five miles south of Flaming Gorge, the Green River enters a broad valley called Brown's Park, now the location of Brown's Park National Wildlife Refuge. The river follows the valley into northwest Colorado, on the northern tip of Dinosaur National Monument.

Brown's Park was originally called Brown's Hole by the fur trappers. Comanche, Shoshoni, and Ute Indians lived there, and Arapaho, Blackfoot, Cheyenne, and Sioux may have hunted there as well. Much later, outlaw Butch Cassidy and assassin Tom Horn used the remote area as a haven.

Brown's Hole is followed by Echo Park, so named because it will rebound an echo of up to ten shouted words off its smooth canyon walls. At the end of the park, the Yampa River enters the Green at the northern tip of what is now Dinosaur National Monument, what Frederick Dellenbaugh, 17-year-old artist and topographer on Powell's second expedition, called "the most striking gorge, next to the Grand Canyon, on the whole river." Dellenbaugh said, "It is 20 miles of concentrated water-power energy and grandeur, the fall being about 400 feet, the walls 2,700. Never for a moment does it relax its assault, and the voyager on its restless, relentless tide, especially at high water, is kept on the alert." Dellenbaugh said that the fearful rush of the river reminded John Wesley Powell of a poem written by Robert Southey in 1820, "The Cataract of Lodore."

No longer as wild as when Powell visited, the Green River meanders through the Lodore Canyon on its way to Dinosaur National Monument.

...Till, in this rapid race
  On which it is bent,
  It reaches the place
  Of its steep descent.

The cataract strong
Then plunges along,
Striking and raging
As if a war waging
Its caverns and rocks among...

Lodore, what Powell's men called "the enemy," was conquered, and the expedition floated on to calmer waters. The river got flatter, wider, and slower, and gave the boatmen a rest.

Dinosaur National Monument

Spread out over 210,000 acres across the Utah and Colorado border, Dinosaur National Monument is one of those out-of-the way gems of America's national park system. Interstate 80 is more than 120 miles north, so you really have to make an effort to visit here, but it's definitely worth the trip.

During the late Jurassic epoch, an ancient river flowed east to west through this area, not northeast to southwest as the Green River does now. More than 150 million years ago, sauropod dinosaurs, the ones with long necks, long tails, small heads, and tree-trunk shaped legs, lived around what is now the northern Utah/Colorado border. Eventually, a long drought killed many of the dinosaurs, and their bodies rotted in and around the dry riverbed. When big rains returned, floods drowned more dinosaurs and the strong currents carried their bones downstream. As the floods diminished, the bones sank into the river to be covered with mud and sand. The result was a dinosaur bone pile-up where Dinosaur National Monument is today.

In 1909, paleontologist Earl Douglass from the Carnegie Museum in Pittsburgh found tall sauropod bones sticking up out of the ground here. Fossils of more than 400 individual dinosaurs from eleven different species were unearthed at this site, and another hundred dinosaurs, totaling more than 1,500 bones, still await excavation.

ABOVE~Steamboat Rock in Echo Park at the confluence of the Yampa and Green rivers in Colorado's section of Dinosaur National Monument.

OVERLEAF~The Green River running true to its name through the Gates of Lodore, in northwestern Colorado.

At the Quarry Site, a huge two-story building with walls made of windows, visitors are awestruck by the "Wall of Bones," the main layer of Douglass's find.

Outside the building in the space between the park entryway and the information center, you can look across a flat plain and see the wide, muddy, Green River meandering its way southwest for about a hundred miles. After that peaceful passage, it plummets into canyons deeper than the Grand Canyon. The Green River drops an amazing 3,000 feet from the time it leaves Flaming Gorge Reservoir at 6,000 feet above sea level until it joins with the Colorado River in Canyon-lands National Park below Moab, Utah, less than two hundred miles away.

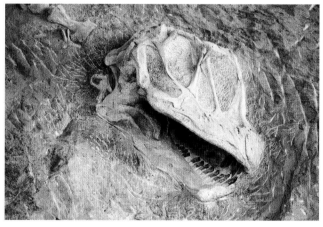

Vernal, Utah, Loves Dinosaurs

The town of Vernal, Utah, is aptly named. It's from the Latin for spring-time, and the town is surrounded by broad green meadows and aspen groves. Vernal lies in Ashley Valley, named after William Henry Ashley, the founder of the Rocky Mountain Fur Company, one of the first An-glos to float the Green River.

There are two gigantic dinosaur statues in downtown Vernal. The big pink one at the east edge of town holds a sign that says, "Vernal, Utah's Dinosaur Land." However, most of the businesses, especially cafes and motels, do most of their trade with fishermen and those staying overnight before embarking on river trips, not with tourists coming to see the dino-saurs. Recently, Vernal has become a mountain biking mecca as well.

TOP~These petroglyphs created by the Fremont culture (AD 1–1200) are located not far from the Dinosaur National Park visitor center.

ABOVE~This Camarasaurus skull, from a Late Jurassic Period plant-eating dino-saur, is on display at the Quarry Exhibit Hall at Dinosaur National Monument.

What happened to the *Brontosaurus*?

Driving around Vernal, one sees several Sinclair gas stations with their green dinosaur logo. At the Chicago World's Fair in 1933, the company presented a dinosaur exhibit, claiming that most oil reserves were created during the Mesozoic Era, when dinosaurs roamed the earth.

Actually, it wasn't dead dinosaurs but million-ton colonies of micro-scopic bacteria and plankton that developed in the oceans three billion years ago that created the oil. They died, sunk to the bottom, and were covered with mud and sand. Temperature and pressure increased on top of them for millions of years, creating what we call oil.

But people loved the exhibit, and Sinclair created Bronty, a big green *Brontosaurus*, as their mascot. They brought him back for the New York World's Fair in 1964, perpetuating the incorrect theory for the next generation of young Baby Boomers.

Then another problem developed. Scientists began to say that there never was a species of dinosaur called a *Brontosaurus*, and that it was just another skeleton of the *Apatosaurus*, both discovered in the same year by paleontologist Othniel Charles Marsh in his race to discover more species than his rival, Edward Cope.

Because *Apatosaurus* was discovered first, that was the name scientists chose. *Brontosaurus* was still used as a synonym, and appeared in books and museum labels. But when the U.S. Postal Service came out with a stamp labeled *Brontosaurus*, hardcore dinosaur fans protested.

To make matters worse, it was discovered about that time that "Bronty" also had the wrong head. There was no skull found for the famous Yale reconstruction of the first *Brontosaurus*, so a head found at another location was used. The correct skull had a longer snout, not the familiar almost-round head portrayed for *Brontosaurus* reconstructions since the early 1900s.

And the controversy isn't over yet. A 2015 study analyzed 81 sauropod specimens from museums all over the world, and the evidence suggests that *Brontosaurus* was indeed a separate species after all. Some scientists are not yet convinced, but those of us who grew up with the name would be pleased to see the return of the *Brontosaurus*.

The Deep Canyons of the Green River

About forty miles southwest of Dinosaur National Monument, where the broad river passes through arid flatlands, lies the small unincorporated community of Ouray, Utah (not to be confused with Ouray, Colorado). Nestled amid sediment-layered hills, it is probably the last relatively easy place to get in or out of the Green River for almost 120 miles.

About eighty miles south of Ouray, the river begins to plunge into Desolation Canyon, whose walls tower 5,000 feet (1,524 m) at some points. At almost eighty-three miles long, Desolation is the longest and deepest canyon that the Green River runs through. It is said to be one of the most remote areas in the continental United States.

How Did All These Canyons Get Here?

The geography for this stretch of the Green River has remained relatively unchanged for millions of years. River drainage in this part of the American West was from south to north 65 to 31 million years ago during the first half of the Tertiary period. The Little Colorado River

TOP~Sunset glowing on Desolation Canyon cliffs with a Green River slough in the foreground.

BOTTOM~Fremont culture petroglyphs in Desolation Canyon.

OPPOSITE~This fossilized sea bed with the Green River in the background is in Desolation Canyon, Utah.

was a major watercourse that flowed from south to north from northern Arizona up to Wyoming. Then 20 to 25 million years ago, during the mid- to late-Miocene epoch, uplifts in northern Colorado and southern Wyoming changed river flow directions dramatically for both the Green and the Colorado rivers. With the rise of the Rockies (initiated tens of millions of years earlier), the prehistoric Colorado now flowed west into Utah. Eventually, the Colorado would change its flow again, heading south to Grand Lake.

At the same time, the Tavaputs Plateau began to uplift as the south side of the Uintah Basin began to rise, affecting the flow of the Green River. The Yampa River began cutting through 4,000 feet of sedimentary rock eroded from the newly risen Rocky Mountains, the relatively soft sandstone Wasatch Formation, and shale (Green River Formation), carving the deep Desolation Canyon as it went. At the same time, the Wind River Range also underwent a new uplift, forcing the Green River to flow south. As the plateau rose, the river cut through it like a knife in the center of a rising loaf of bread, with Desolation Canyon separating the two halves.

LEFT~Sandstone cliffs in Gray Canyon.

OPPOSITE~A leafy yellow canopy frames Gunnison Butte on the Green River.

Gray Canyon and Beyond

After Desolation Canyon comes Gray Canyon, formerly called Coal Canyon. Gray is narrower than Desolation, and taken together they make up a popular multiday floating trip. The two canyons are known for their easy rapids, and depending on weather conditions and time of year, most of the trip is flat and peaceful.

The Green River leaves Gray Canyon just above the town of Green River, Utah, and flows through an open area for about thirty miles, passing calmly through the town before entering Labyrinth and Stillwater canyons, the last of the canyons it traverses before joining the Colorado River. These are quiet canyons, where the river snakes its wide arcs around red sandstone cliffs. The two canyons run 123 miles, where at the end of Stillwater Canyon, the Green River meets the Colorado in the heart of Canyonlands National Park.

Green River, Utah

Like the other town named Green River, in Wyoming, the most important reason for the founding of Green River, Utah, is its location as a natural landing on a calm flat stretch of the river where boatmen can get on and off the river easily.

LEFT~Book Cliffs in Gray Canyon were named by an imaginative explorer for their resemblance to a shelf full of books.

BELOW~The seeds are as big as hubcaps on this giant slice of watermelon in Green River, Utah.

What eventually became the town of Green River was part of the Old Spanish Trail trade route from 1829 up until the 1850s, and the optimistic "Green River City" started as a U.S. Post Office at the river crossing. The population boomed as workers arrived to build a bridge across the river for the Denver and Rio Grande Western Railroad in the early 1880s. Then the town became a water and fuel stop, and the Palmer House Hotel served railroad workers and travelers.

Uranium mining played a major part in the town's economy from the 1940s through the 1960s. Several trucking companies hauled ore from mines west of Green River. Today, because it is located about one hundred miles west of Grand Junction, Colorado, and one hundred miles east of Richfield, Utah, Green River's primary economy centers on Interstate 70 traffic. Green River is also known as a popular mountain biking area, and an organizing spot for river trips.

Green River is also famous for its melons. They celebrate the harvest with "Melon Days," in September. The festival's 25-foot-long trailer, shaped and painted to look like a giant watermelon, was featured in *Ripley's Believe It Or Not*.

On the east edge of town, actually located on the east bank of the Green River, is the John Wesley Powell Museum. The museum exhibits focus on Major John Wesley Powell's Colorado River expeditions, but there are also excellent displays describing the geography, geology, and dinosaurs.

About four and a half miles downstream (southwest) of town near the east bank of the river is Crystal Geyser, a rare example of a cold water geyser. The groundwater in the area contains large amounts of carbon dioxide, and there are substantial pockets of subsurface gas as well. The carbon dioxide creates enough pressure to force water out of the ground to heights of up to 131 feet (40 m). The geyser often erupts every eight hours, but sometimes every twenty-two hours. Eruptions last anywhere from seven minutes to two hours.

Labyrinth Canyon, Stillwater Canyon, and the Confluence

From the town of Green River to its confluence with the Colorado River, the Green River flows about 120 miles through Labyrinth and Stillwater canyons. These canyons are much alike, with sandstone walls that rise almost straight up as high as 1,300 feet (396 m) above the river.

About twenty-four miles south of the town, the Green River enters Labyrinth Canyon, 68 river miles (110 km) long. Labyrinth Canyon includes Bowknot Bend, an almost 360-degree hairpin reverse. It goes past Mineral Bottom, and after several more switchbacks around the cliffs, Labyrinth merges into Stillwater Canyon, with a view of a rock formation called Cleopatra's Chair, at an elevation of 6,250 feet (1,905 m). The Panorama Overlook, at 6,240 feet (1,902 m), is only a few miles to the east of the chair.

The Green River joins the Colorado River in Stillwater Canyon at an elevation of 3,855 feet (1,487 m). The two equal-sized rivers come from either side of a tall mesa and combine into one big Colorado River that goes south from there. From above, it looks like a giant wishbone, or maybe a slingshot.

So there you have the Green River, from its rivulets trickling from the Wind River Range glaciers to clear mountain lakes, lush rangelands, arid prairies, and some of the deepest canyons in the United States. It is a formidable river by any standard, both in length and volume, but once it joins with Colorado, of equal size and strength, they become "The Mighty Colorado."

Moving on down the Green River, Labyrinth Canyon in Canyonlands National Park.

Chapter 2

The Colorado from Its Source to the Confluence

OPPOSITE~Summertime is a constant cascade of crystal clear water in Rocky Mountain National Park near Estes Park, Colorado.

BELOW~Five miles below its source at La Poudre Lake, the Colorado River is not very wide as it rushes down the west side of the Rocky Mountains.

The Source of the Colorado River

Like the Green River, and all large rivers, the Colorado begins high in the mountains. In this case, it's high on the west side of the Rocky Mountains, the largest mountain range in the United States. The Rockies stretch more than 3,000 miles from Canada to New Mexico, and are home to more than fifty peaks higher than 14,000 feet (4,267 m).

Rivers are made up of high mountain snowflakes that melt into water droplets, which merge into trickles, like raindrops running down a car windshield. Purists say that you have to climb the peaks until you can't hear water flowing. That's where the river really starts.

But the official source of the Colorado River is La Poudre Pass Lake (pronounced "pooder"), a little lake a few miles below La Poudre Pass, elevation 10,184 feet (3,104 m). From the wet meadows south of the flat, swampy pass, newly formed La Poudre Creek flows east, eventually joining the Mississippi River. Meanwhile, thirty miles away on the other side of the Continental Divide, the Colorado River begins, heading south and west 1,450 miles (2,334 m) to the Gulf of California.

La Poudre Lake is only about sixteen miles west-northwest of Estes Park, Colorado, as the crow flies, but the road from one point to the other is ninety miles long. And even then, you can only travel there from July to September, depending on weather conditions. The name of the lake comes from the nearby Cache la Poudre River, which flows east down the Front Range of the Rockies. In the 1820s, French fur trappers were caught in a snowstorm alongside the river and had to bury a portion of their gunpowder supply there because it was too heavy to carry. The phrase Cache la Poudre translates to "hide the powder." All of these places—pass, lake, and rivers, are within the boundaries of Rocky Mountain National Park.

All About Glaciers

According to the experts at Rocky Mountain National Park, a glacier is a mass of snow and ice that exists all year round. It is large enough and heavy enough to flow as slow as molasses in January. When more snow accumulates each year than is lost by melting and evaporation, a glacier is formed. It continues to grow and spread, moving downhill as new snow accumulates and condenses the old snow into dense blue ice. Glaciers are a beautifully pale translucent blue because water molecules absorb other colors better, and also because the dense ice squeezes out air bubbles, which normally make ordinary ice look white. When light passes through thick ice, all the colors of the spectrum are absorbed except blue.

When glaciers stop flowing downhill, they are said to retreat. This sounds like they have reversed direction and are now moving uphill, but that's not true. When more snow melts than is replaced over several years, a glacier shrinks, or "retreats." My grandfather was a Yankee farmer, and he loved to tell the story about the city visitor who saw a farmer removing rocks from his field.

"Where'd all those rocks come from," the city man asked.

"The glaciers brought 'em," replied the farmer.

The visitor continued, "I don't see any glaciers. Where are they now?"

"Well," said the farmer, "They went back to get more rocks."

Currently, the only glaciers in Rocky Mountain National Park are small cirque glaciers. These arcs of ice are found in mostly shaded round basins at the upper end of mountain valleys, and are usually the remains of larger Little Ice Age valley glaciers, which filled several Rocky Mountain valleys 700 to 165 years ago.

In addition to glaciers, the Rockies near the source of the Colorado River are also home to perennial snowfields, which never melt completely but are not thick enough to compress snow crystals to form glacial ice. The flow of the Colorado River parallels a range called the "Never Summer Mountains," since there is snow there all year around.

OPPOSITE~Glaciers in the appropriately named Never Summer Mountains feed water into the rapidly growing Colorado River near its source.

ABOVE~Summer at the top of the Rockies, where ancient rocks meet never-melting snow in Rocky Mountain National Park. It's obvious why the state of Colorado chose a view like this for their automobile license plates.

Why the Rocky Mountains Deserve a Park

There's a reason that tourists, especially those visiting from other countries, choose to visit our country's national parks before they see anything else. Visiting national parks is like following a restaurant guide. Some knowledgeable group of people has already explored what's out there, and presented you with the most fascinating places to visit.

Since Congress designated Yellowstone National Park in 1872 "as a public park or pleasuring ground for the benefit and enjoyment of the people," many government officials, state and local leaders, and ordinary citizens have worked to set aside lands that "are of such national significance as to justify special recognition and protection in accordance with various acts of Congress."

The Rocky Mountains, one of the most spectacular mountain ranges in the world, certainly merits that "national significance." Almost all mountain ranges all over the world, including parts of the Rockies, form where two tectonic plates jam together and one rises up while the other one slides steeply underneath. Not so with the Rocky Mountains' Foreland Ranges of Colorado, however, which encompass Rocky Mountain National Park. These curious ranges rose up in the middle of the continent, hundreds of miles from any plate edges. Recent data suggest to geologists that a piece of the east-moving ocean plate (the Farallon Plate),

LEFT~First light warming the Moraine Valley near Estes Park, Colorado.

OPPOSITE~Wind-blown snow and Long's Peak in the background, a view from Trail Ridge Road.

BELOW~Just your typical yellow-bellied marmots on the lookout for trouble.

being lightweight, subducted nearly flat far inland, beneath Colorado, like a board sliding under a rug. By seventy million years ago, the Farallon Plate bumped up huge blocks of ancient ocean-bottom sediments and billion-year-old metamorphic rock and granite to great heights, to create Colorado's high, enigmatic Foreland mountain ranges.

There are now more than four hundred national parks and monuments in the United States, totalling 84 million acres under the care of the National Park Service in all fifty states and affiliated areas. As if to say it's among the best of the best, Rocky Mountain National Park is the fifth most visited national park, and for good reason. Located about seventy-seven miles northwest of Denver, Colorado, Rocky Mountain National Park's 415 square miles encompass spectacular mountain environments, more than three hundred miles of hiking trails, and beautiful alpine wildflowers, plus close-up views of elk, Rocky Mountain bighorn sheep, and even marmots. Yellow-bellied marmots are large alpine squirrels, also called mountain mice even though they are the size of a small house cat. They hibernate about five months of the year, from September/early October to early April or May.

From one of the entrances to Rocky Mountain National Park at Beaver Meadows, 7,840 feet (2,390 m) above sea level, the park's mountains rise to their highest point of 14,259 feet (4,346 m) at the top of Longs Peak. Thin mountain air is a serious concern for humans at elevations above 9,000 feet. At 14,000 feet, for instance, the air has 39 percent less oxygen than at sea level. Breathing and heart rate increase, and some people experience headaches, fatigue, and nausea, known as "mountain sickness."

Trail Ridge Road

Trail Ridge Road is without a doubt the most scenic road in North America. If you love to drive, you will not find a more exhilarating experience than motoring up Trail Ridge Road, one of the highest and, at 47 miles long, the longest continuously paved high-altitude road in the continental United States. It starts at 7,522 feet (2,292 m) at Estes Park, Colorado, in a montane ecosystem full of ponderosa pine forests populated with beaver, elk, and squirrels.

In less than half an hour, the road climbs above 9,000 feet into a subalpine zone of more sparsely situated spruce and fir trees, with open mountain meadows and breathtaking views of big black snow-capped mountains that look like reclining pandas in their black and white fur coats. Along the sides of the road, melting snow freshets rush down the mountainsides and across the road, even in late June.

The map says it takes only forty-seven minutes to get to the Alpine Visitor Center at the crest of the road, but that doesn't take into account the many stops along the way to view herds of elk, Rocky Mountain bighorn sheep, and feathery ptarmigans in high mountain meadows and snowy valley slopes.

The white-tailed ptarmigan, also called a snow hen, lives only above the tree line, and is the smallest species of grouse in North America. Its plumage is gray and brown in the summer, but fades to reddish gray in the fall as it begins to grow white feathers. By winter, all the colored feathers have dropped out and the bird is completely white. It molts again in the spring, dropping the white feathers and growing brown ones once again. Ptarmigans are the only birds that live on the tundra all year round without hibernating, as does a small rabbit relative, the pika.

Finally, the sign at one of the scenic views says that you are standing at 12,100 feet (3,688 m), the most easily accessible alpine tundra region in the world. From the parking lot, you have a tremendous view of four hundred miles of treeless black mountains made up of rocks from the earth's crustal basement that are more than a billion years old.

ABOVE~White-tailed ptarmigan in winter plumage.

LEFT~Alpine sunflowers along Trail Ridge Road, Rocky Mountain National Park.

Alpine Visitor Center

You are driving along on top of mountain ridges above 11,000 feet and you haven't seen any conveniences on the road since Estes Park, except the parking lots of scenic viewpoints. Who would expect to find the large, beautiful Alpine Visitor Center, where you can look out the two-story plate glass windows to view the "Land with no Trees" from the comfort of their bookstore, gift shop, and café? And they even have an espresso bar! The center is open from late May to early October, and you can see extraordinary views of the tundra and the Fall River Cirque (permanent snowfield) from there.

Displays at the center describe alpine tundra ecology, including two unusual critters at home on the tundra. Marmots can sometimes be seen alongside Trail Ridge Road and at the scenic viewpoints. Listen closely for the shy pika. Pikas, also called coneys, or rock rabbits, give out a shrill alarm when they perceive danger, giving them the nickname "whistling hare."

The pika is a small, round-bodied animal, named by the Tungus people of eastern Manchuria.

Lulu City Strikes It Not So Rich

Because of its remote mountain location, the only community that ever attempted to grow near the source of the Colorado River was Lulu City, where hundreds of prospectors rushed in after silver was discovered there in 1879. The town was named after mine investor Captain Benjamin F. Burnett's daughter, who was born on May 13, 1871. At its peak, the town had a large hotel, a store, several saloons, forty cabins, and a small red-light district. Lulu Burnett's town was on the river just three miles south of the headwaters. But the ore was not rich enough to warrant the high cost of getting it down off the mountain, so Lulu City's post office closed in 1886 and the town was abandoned, except for one lone prospector, Joe Shipler, who had discovered the first traces of silver there.

A few other mining communities struggled for a while, but building a town on top of a mountain was not practical. Plus, the big gold and silver discoveries were farther south at Cherry Creek, Cripple Creek, and Leadville. One of those historic alpine communities that made it into the 21st century, however, is Estes Park, Colorado, at the gateway to Rocky Mountain National Park.

Estes Park, Colorado

Because of its fair climate, Estes Park has a long history, and a prehistory as well. Archaeological evidence indicates the first people to live in the area were from the Clovis Culture, around 12,000 years ago. By 2000 BC, a Paleo-Indian group called the McKean people hunted there. Families of Ute and Arapaho Indians began to spend their summers in the area about 2,000 years ago. They wintered just south of Grand Lake, and there is still evidence of the trail they took over the Continental Divide in Rocky Mountain National Park.

Because it was easier to reach the Front Range of the Rockies from the already settled territories, Euro-American history begins a little earlier there. Major Stephen H. Long led a group of mountain men into the Rockies in 1820, several years before Ashley's company reached the Green River, Wyoming, area. Here, the similarities between the alpine communities of Pinedale, Wyoming, and Estes Park, Colorado, diverge.

The California Gold Rush changed the world in 1849 by providing instant riches for adventurous prospectors, but ten years later most of the easy pickings were gone and prospectors turned elsewhere to strike it rich. Starting in 1859 with Pikes Peak and lasting into the early 1860s, the Front Range of the Rocky Mountains, including Denver, Leadville, Aspen, and Cripple Creek, is considered to be one of the largest gold and silver rushes in American history.

Most of the discoveries were farther south, but John Estes, a Kentuckian who struck it rich in California, tried prospecting in the area in 1859, so it was named after him. He brought his wife and thirteen children the following year.

Millions of people have enjoyed vacations in Estes Park for more than a century, including Pope John Paul II, the Emperor of Japan, and President George W. Bush. The entrances to Rocky Mountain National Park are just a few minutes west of Estes Park.

Fresh snow above Forest Canyon, with Long's Peak in the background.

The Other Front Range

In addition to being the name of the eastern slopes of the Rocky Mountains, the Front Range is so named because it was the first range reached by explorers after crossing the Great Plains. Front Range is also a local geographic name for the most-populated area in Colorado.

The Green River and Colorado River were both created by uplifting plateaus, and they both focus on hunting and fishing in the north and boating and water skiing in the south. Population, however, is where they differ greatly. The area around the Green River is sparsely populated, and always has been. On the other hand, the Front Range has been much more densely populated since the 1860s.

The difference, it seems, was location, location, location. Today, the Front Range of the Rockies shields the foothill communities from major storm conditions. More than a century ago, there was a different attraction: tourism, hunting, and fishing. It was much faster for well-to-do New Yorkers, Chicagoans, and Europeans to get off the train in Denver one day and be high up in the Rockies the next day. Like the upper Green River, the upper Colorado is a fly fisherman's paradise. On the other side of the pass from the Colorado River, there are large populations of brown trout in the Cache la Poudre River.

While most of the interest and population is on the east side of the Rockies, the river goes down the west side. Heading west from the Alpine Visitor Center, Trail Ridge Road begins to follow the Colorado River. This trip from Estes Park west over the Continental Divide would have taken days, if not weeks, before the convenience of today's paved roads and bridges.

> And the Colorado rocky mountain high,
> I've seen it raining fire in the sky,
> I know he'd be a poorer man if he never saw an eagle fly,
> rocky mountain high.
>
> —JOHN DENVER, "Rocky Mountain High"

Grand Lake, Colorado

The town of Grand Lake was established in 1881 at an elevation of 8,369 feet (2,551 m) as a supply point for mining towns and camps like Lulu City. Now it's a tourist destination and gateway to the western entrance of Rocky Mountain National Park, which borders the lake on three sides. Because it's only a few hours away from Denver, Grand Lake is a more upscale summer getaway than you would find in Wyoming. It has a repertory theater, condos, and a lakeside hotel with tennis courts and a heated swimming pool. And Grand Lake, less than two miles wide or long, is the largest natural body of water in Colorado. Downriver a few miles, and often less crowded, the Lake Granby area is a popular spot for winter skiing and salmon and trout fishing the rest of the year. From there, the easiest way to follow the river is to take Highway 40 west out of Granby, then south seventy-three miles to the junction with Interstate 70, then thirty miles west to Vail, Colorado.

Sailboating on Grand Lake, eighteen miles south of the Colorado River headwaters.

Interstate 70—The Colorado River Route

Rocky Mountain passes are rugged, steep, and narrow. That's why Interstate 70 is the largest, and nearly the only, road that connects Denver to Colorado's major ski resorts. Because water usually seeks the easiest path on its journey from alpine mountains to the sea, it makes sense that Interstate 70 follows the Colorado River for several hundred miles through Colorado.

Fifty miles west of Denver, the Eisenhower-Johnson Memorial Tunnel burrows under the Continental Divide at an elevation of 11,158 feet (3,401 m), making it the highest point on the Interstate Highway System. It is also the longest mountain tunnel and one of the world's highest vehicular underpasses. The tunnel is named after President Dwight D. Eisenhower and former Colorado governor and U.S. Senator Edwin C. Johnson. Because the highway passes through this tunnel, then through Glenwood Canyon and the San Rafael Swell, Interstate 70 is considered a major engineering marvel.

Vail, Colorado

Outside of Switzerland, Vail, Colorado, is probably the most famous ski area in the world. Back Bowls, Bear Tree, Born Free, Blue Sky Basin, Lodgepole, Riva Ridge, and Simba—these are just a few of the dozens, if not hundreds, of ski areas looming above the city of Vail, nestled beneath Vail Mountain in the Gore Valley. Just a hundred miles from Denver via Interstate 70, Vail is one of the most accessible ski areas in the United States. With more than 5,000 acres of ski country, Vail has been the winter haven for snowboarders and ski fanatics for more than half a century.

Basking in sunny days for almost three hundred days a year, Vail is also known for deluxe accommodations, fine dining, chic shopping, and luxurious spas. Despite its opulence, Vail is a hub for serious skiers as well; it was the home of the 2015 World Alpine Ski Championships, and the U.S. Ski Team trains there.

Mountain goat and kid, high atop the Rockies.

The Lost Horse Mill on the Crystal River, just south of Glenwood Springs, Colorado.

Glenwood Springs, Colorado

Glenwood Springs sits right alongside the Colorado River, but it is a town of many faces, not just another river town. The area surrounding Glenwood Springs was originally inhabited by the nomadic Ute Indians who lived in parts of Utah, Colorado, New Mexico, and Wyoming. The name Ute means "land of the sun."

Though Glenwood Springs is a river town, with rafting adventure outfits on almost every corner, it's also a spa town because of its natural hot springs. Once the railroad arrived in 1887, it was easy for the wealthy to visit what became a popular resort town, which made it a favorite jumping-off place for presidents, fishermen, hunters, and skiers, and a perfect summer getaway for tourists. In addition to tourism, the local economy was fueled by coal mining, ranching, and outdoor recreation.

But most of all, Glenwood Springs was originally a farm town, celebrated by its Strawberry Days festival the third weekend in June every year for more than 180 years. The residents of the mining towns of Aspen and Leadville needed a steady supply of food at reasonable prices to keep their communities going. According to one of many historic labels posted on downtown buildings, watermelons grew to an "astounding size, with crisp flesh of exceedingly fine flavor." Large alfalfa fields were necessary to feed the growing number of cattle raised in the area as well.

Farming looks mighty easy when your plow is a pencil, and you're a thousand miles from the cornfield.

—PRESIDENT DWIGHT D. EISENHOWER

The Springs in Glenwood

Swedish immigrant Jonas Lindgren came to the Glenwood Springs area in 1881. He found relief for his arthritis at a large hot spring that gushed forth near the banks of the Colorado River. Lindgren built a big wooden bathtub and filled it with hot mineral water, then tempered the heat with buckets of cool river water. Word soon spread, and miners from Leadville and Aspen sought relief at a dime per bath.

The population grew, and more and more bathers wanted to soak in the therapeutic waters. On Independence Day, 1888, a six-hundred-foot-long hot-springs pool opened for high-class health seekers. The pool and bathhouse were made of fine-grained reddish-colored sandstone known as Peachblow, quarried from the banks of the Frying Pan River. President Benjamin Harrison's party enjoyed the pool there in about 1891. The hot springs pool and stone bathhouse are still there—"the gateway to the spa in the mountains."

Surfing in Landlocked Colorado?

The first of its kind in the state of Colorado, the Glenwood Springs Whitewater Activity Area is an unusual destination for paddling, kayaking, and surfing enthusiasts from around the world. "The Wave," as some locals call it, was completed in 2008. The main feature is a standing wave, a constant stationary wave on the Colorado River, created artificially with strategically placed rocks and concrete. At this section of the river in West Glenwood not far from Interstate 70, surfers face upstream and catch the wave, which allows them to surf against it for as long as they can keep their balance, giving the feeling of traveling fast over water while not actually moving, like a surfer treadmill.

The Hotel Colorado

Built in 1893, the Hotel Colorado offered a European-style spa to serve the wealthy, often newly minted mining millionaires.

President Theodore Roosevelt stayed at the hotel several times, starting when he was vice president in 1901. President McKinley was assassinated on September 14, 1901, and Roosevelt became president. Roosevelt was elected president in 1904, and stayed at the Hotel Colorado for three weeks in 1905 while he went bear hunting in the surrounding mountains. President William Howard Taft stayed there as well. Asked if he would care to use the hot springs pool, Taft said, "I've found it's much better for a man of my size not to bathe in public."

Kayaker working "The Wave," a man-made feature on the Colorado River in West Glenwood Springs.

The Wave is a perfect spot for surfers and kayakers to practice because they can ride the Wave all day without any down time. No need to search for waves or chase after them, it's always there at the same place. The park was selected for the 2009 U.S. Freestyle Kayaking Team Trials in 2009, and is often host to the Rocky Mountain Surf Festival.

Meanwhile, the Colorado River gets stronger, wider, and redder as other rivers feed into it.

On Down the River...

Rivers adding to the Colorado River from its source to Grand Junction and beyond to the confluence include the Williams Fork, Blue, Eagle, Roaring Fork, and the Gunnison rivers. Many of the upper tributaries are small, but the Roaring Fork and Gunnison contribute massive amounts of water.

By the time it reaches the Utah border, the Colorado varies between 200 to 1,200 feet (60 to 370 m) wide, and anywhere from six to thirty feet deep. Near Fruita, Colorado, just west of Grand Junction, the Colorado flows southwest and is met by the Dolores River just across the Utah border. The Colorado then borders part of Arches National Park a few miles west of Moab, Utah, curves around Deadhorse Point State Park, then flows south through Canyonlands National Park, where it meets its major tributary, the Green River.

Land's End Observatory on top of Grand Mesa, the largest flat-topped mountain in the world. Near Grand Junction, Colorado, the building was designed by the Works Progress Administration (WPA) to appear as though it was growing out of the earth.

OVERLEAF: Colorado National Monument, below Grand Junction, Colorado, thirty-two square miles of scenic wonders.

Grand Junction, Colorado

One of Grand Junction's nicknames is "River City," and for good reason. It got the name Grand because it's on the Grand River, renamed the Colorado in 1921. It got the second half of the name, Junction, because the Gunnison River joins the Colorado here from the south.

It is the largest city on the western slope of the Rockies, and a major transportation hub for the vast open spaces reaching east to the Rockies and west to the Green River.

Like almost every location on the Green and Colorado rivers, the area's first inhabitants, dating back to 11,000 BCE, were Paleo-Indians. Archaic Indians followed, 8,000 BCE to 500 AD, and began to experiment with farming. The Fremont Culture, 700 to 1200 AD, lived in caves and then pit houses. Their petroglyphs and pictographs can be found from Dinosaur National Park near the Wyoming border, to Arches National Park in southern Utah, eighty miles east to Grand Junction,

and a little bit into Nevada to the west. The Ute tribe, who hunted throughout Utah and Colorado and did some seasonal farming, superseded the prehistoric cultures.

Grand Junction is also known as the capital of Colorado's wine country. Grand Valley, stretching twenty-five miles along Interstate 70 from Palisade on the east, through Grand Junction in the middle, to Fruita on the west edge, nurtures more than twenty wineries and vineyards in the shadows of the surrounding red rock cliffs and mesas. At 4,700 feet above sea level, the grapes get intense heat and sun almost every day of the year without the cold winters found just up the road at Glenwood Springs. It is also a relatively dry climate, perfect for growing grapes.

About twelve miles west of Grand Junction, about halfway to the Colorado/Utah border, the town of Fruita gives a good example of the importance of agriculture to the area. More recently, Fruita has become famous for its world-class mountain biking trails. Kokopelli Trail is 142 miles (229 km) long and often follows old Jeep trails up, around, and over the high-desert red-rock mesas and into gullies in continuous single- and double-track trails.

The river bends at Fruita, and seven miles directly south of the town is the Colorado National Monument. To the west of the monument, the Colorado River winds diagonally southwest through the McInnes Canyon National Conservation Area.

Colorado Plateau

Just as the Green River sliced down through the rising sedimentary rock of the Tavaputs Plateau in Utah, carving deep inaccessible gorges, the rising Colorado Plateau caused the Colorado River to do the same thing in southwestern Colorado, then southwest to Arches National Park. Once the Green and Colorado rivers join at that location, the business of cutting canyons through rising plateaus begins in earnest.

Bridge over the Gunnison River at Grand Junction.

The Colorado Plateau covers 140,000 miles of the Four Corners area of Arizona, Colorado, New Mexico, and Utah. In addition to the Colorado and Green rivers, it includes areas drained by the San Juan and Little Colorado rivers.

The plateau is primarily high desert with a few scattered forests. It is a land of barren badlands, deep canyons, mesas, and plateaus, with sparse outcroppings of sage, juniper, desert mallow, and brittlebrush. Unhampered by the distances, adapting to the lack of water, and thriving on the scarcity of human populations, eagles, desert mountain sheep, coyotes, rabbits, and a wide variety of desert birds and bugs live there.

Its nickname, "Red Rock Country" refers to the brightly colored sandstone, easily seen because arid climate and sparse vegetation help speed up erosion on the bare cliffs and mesas. As a result, the plateau is home to nature's best rock sculpture galleries of hoodoos, natural bridges, slot canyons, and much more.

The "basement" of the Colorado Plateau, seen mostly in the bottom of the Grand Canyon, is made up of ancient Precambrian rocks. They are mostly metamorphic rocks formed over a billion years ago deep in the earth, as tectonic plates collided to create continents. Millions of years later, lava and magma flowed into them and solidified into igneous rocks, forming a marbled layer of metamorphic rocks. Sediments deposited on this hard basement formed the layered and tiled Precambrian

Sunlight and snow, Canyonlands National Park near Moab, Utah.

Green River Overlook, Canyonlands National Park.

sedimentary units exposed sporadically throughout the Grand Canyon. The rock layers rose up, eroded back down, and by 600 million years ago were polished smooth. During the Paleozoic era (542 to 251 million years ago), tropical seas flooded the area, and thick layers of sedimentary limestone, mudstone, sandstone, and shale formed deposits on top of the ancient granite and Vishnu Schist.

From one geological epoch to another, layer after layer of limestone, mudstone, sandstone, and shale settled to the bottom of the ocean, creating a giant sandstone parfait. Then, over millions of years, tectonic forces moving the earth's crust caused this giant block of sediments, thousands of feet thick in some places, to raise, twist, and sink back down. Lava flowed over them, and wind and water wore them away.

Geologists' evidence suggests that Navajo Sandstone, one of the thickest layers, is 180 million years old and came from erosion of the Appalachian Mountains, a huge range that now parallels the east coast of the United States from New York to Mississippi. But before the continents drifted to where they are now, the whole block resided much farther south.

With the formation of Pangaea, a supercontinent formed about 300 million years ago from earlier land masses that began to break up and spread apart approximately 175 million years ago, terrestrial deposits were more prevalent than ocean sediments. Giant sand dunes hardened, and volcanic eruptions buried large areas in ash. With the creation of mountains, oceans and lakes filled and dried out, leaving more sediment.

While the Rocky Mountains and the many ranges of the Basin and Range area were being formed, what is now the Colorado Plateau was still a thick block of the earth's crust that had suffered very little breakup from faulting and folding for about 600 million years. Around 65 million years ago during the Cenozoic era when both the Basin and Range region and the Colorado Plateau were about the same low elevation, something happened and geologists still disagree about its cause. Both the Colorado Plateau and the Basin and Range raised up almost two miles (3 km). The Basin and Range broke into many long mountain ranges and valleys, while the Colorado Plateau rose as one block for more than another half mile.

As we have seen with the Tavaputs Plateau, thousands of acres of sedimentary rock formations in the area where Utah, Colorado, New Mexico, and Arizona come together raised more than a thousand feet from their former elevation. This created the Colorado Plateau, and as it rose, the Colorado River cut into it, and less than six million years ago, it carved the Grand Canyon.

There are ten U.S. National Park units and dozens of monuments, state parks, and other natural reserve areas on the Colorado Plateau, more than anywhere else in the United States. Among these are Arches, Canyonlands, and the Grand Canyon, all related to the Colorado River.

Serene reflections on the Colorado River, Canyonlands National Park.

Colorado National Monument

Only a long day's drive from the Rocky's alpine tundra, the scenic views
from Colorado National Monument's Rim Rock Drive seem like they
are from another world. This is the east edge of the mesa lands, stretching west across southern Utah and northern Arizona to the east edge of
Nevada.

Like the deep canyons carved by the Green River in Wyoming and
Utah, here in the monument's thirty-two square miles, the Colorado
River cuts down through the eastern edge of the Colorado Plateau's deep
sandstone to the ancient basement granite, gneiss, and schist to shape
magnificent steep-walled canyons.

Colorado National Monument offers more than forty hiking trails
through its red rock canyons. Serpents Trail is the most popular, but one
of the shortest is Devil's Kitchen. The monument brochure says, "Devil's
Kitchen trail is well-suited for families with smaller children, as the hike
is short and the 'kitchen' itself provides plenty of opportunity for child-
sized exploration."

Near the Utah/Colorado border, twenty miles west of the monument,
the Colorado River drops south in the McInnis Canyons National Conservation Area and ends its approximately 235-mile parallel alongside
Interstate 70. The best place to catch sight of the river again is in Arches
National Park, five miles north of Moab, Utah.

Moab and the Canyons

When is a river town a river town even if it's not on the river? When it's Moab, Utah, of course. It is both five miles south and five miles east of the river, given the snaky nature of the Colorado. But Moab definitely has the independent free-spirited character of a river town. Towns on the upper Green and Colorado are all about hunting, fishing, and skiing, for the most part, while the main attractions for the southern portions are mountain biking, kayaking, rafting, and boating. And, of course, the phenomenal canyons, arches, spires, and scenic vistas make Moab a popular Colorado River tourist destination.

Named by Mormon settler William Pierce after the biblical land beyond the Jordan River in the Middle East, Moab is a fitting appellation for a remote desert river town. In 1830, the Republic of Mexico opened what John C. Fremont later called the Old Spanish Trail between Santa Fe and Los Angeles. Coupled with the Santa Fe Trail, the route created an arduous, nearly impassable transcontinental route from St. Joseph, Missouri, to Los Angeles, California.

There was some tourism in the area as early as 1906, but Moab's remoteness kept it isolated. Then in the 1940s, encouraged by U.S. government bounties, uranium in the surrounding Chinle Foundation sandstone brought on a mining boom. Moab's population mushroomed from 1,275 in 1950 to 4,682 ten years later. However, tourism did not boom until the 1960s when outdoor adventuring took off.

Moab is the gateway to both Arches and Canyonlands national parks, as well as Dead Horse Point State Park, and is near Utah's easiest Colorado River crossing. The area is the putting-in spot for thousands of river-running adventurers, but more recently a favorite destination for mountain bikers. It's not unusual to stand at Moab's main downtown intersection and see trucks hauling boat trailers in one direction and tour vans with more than half a dozen bicycles in racks on the top in another. But the real attractions are the magnificent canyons and incredible arches.

ABOVE~Prince's plume (*Stanleya pinnata*) near Moab, Utah.

BELOW~The Gooseneck at Dead Horse Point State Park, Utah.

Arches National Park

There are more than 2,500 sandstone arches in the park that's named after them, in varying shades of pink, orange, and red. The Colorado River forms most of the southern boundary of the park, but does not play a major role in the arches' creation.

ABOVE~Turret Arch, framed through North Window Arch, Arches National Park, Utah.

BELOW~Delicate Arch with La Sal Mountains in the background, Arches National Park, Utah.

And why are there so many arches in this one place? More than 300 million years ago, as an ancient ocean evaporated, it left behind beds of salt sometimes thousands of feet deep. These were buried under debris and sediment for millions of years. During the early Jurassic period (200 million to 175 million years ago), a layer of Entrada sandstone covered the existing Navajo sandstone. The Entrada layer was then covered with 5,000 feet of sediment, and the pressure of its weight heated the salt deep underneath, which turned to a "plastic" solid that moved somewhat like toothpaste. It pushed up and to the west against existing faults, and moved up into the upper layers, causing domes of piled-up salt beneath the surface. As the earth on top eroded thousands of years later, the salt eroded faster, leaving the arches, which are still being carved by water, wind, and ice.

These amazing arches are such an important part of the state's image—just as the Grand Canyon is to Arizona—that the government put Delicate Arch on the official state license plate. The sixty-five-foot-tall (20 m) Delicate Arch is the most popular one in the park, so much so that in 2002 the Olympic Torch was carried under the arch on its way to the Winter Games in Salt Lake City.

President Herbert Hoover signed legislation making Arches a national monument in 1929. It wasn't until 1971, however, that Congress made it a national park.

The Colorado River forms the southern boundary of the park. At the west edge of Arches National Park, the river turns southward.

Canyonlands National Park

About twenty-five miles southwest of Arches National Park by road, and at least forty winding "river miles," lie almost 340,000 acres of picturesque arches, buttes, canyons, mesas, and spires known as Canyonlands National Park. Situated in the midst of Utah's high desert, Canyonlands is the only area formed by a pair of mighty rivers, the Green and the Colorado.

Before they join, the Green and the Colorado are almost without rapids, leisurely and serene. There is often an interesting difference in the amount of sediment the rivers carry. At one time, one is muddier than the other, and another time the opposite is true. After they join, the two different rivers, one muddy and one clear, flow alongside each other for a while, but with narrows and rapids, they eventually mix.

In the Y-shaped wedge just before the Green and Colorado meet, the formation called Island in the Sky towers over the rivers on sheer sandstone cliffs 2,000 feet (600 m) above them, giving an excellent bird's-eye view of the area. The paved scenic drive has many road pullouts with fantastic long-distance views of the canyons and the rivers.

LEFT~The Green River in Canyonlands National Park, just before it merges with the Colorado.

BELOW~Chesler Park viewpoint is in the Needles District, Canyonlands National Park, Utah.

OPPOSITE: The Colorado River, formerly the Grand River, just before its confluence with the Green River, Canyonlands National Park.

Cataract Canyon

Below the junction of the Grand and the Green,
the augmented water pours down,
a succession of rapids of great pitch and violence,
over falls of sharp-cut rocks, and unbroken rushes
between beachless shores of thousand-foot cliffs.
    — MARY AUSTIN, *The Land of Journey's Ending*, 1924

Several miles downstream from the confluence, the newly blended Colorado surges into Cataract Canyon. There are two different definitions of the word cataract. The one most familiar is an abnormality of the eye, but the second definition comes from a Greek word meaning waterfall, or rushing down.

Cataract Canyon spans Canyonlands National Park and Glen Canyon National Recreation Area, ending with the Colorado River's confluence with the Dirty Devil River, and then it blends into Glen Canyon. Almost half of the last section is now submerged beneath Lake Powell.

Now nearly twice its size, the river heaves into roiling rapids created by rocks and debris dumped by tributaries, landslides, fallen boulders, and piles of rock eroded from the steep cliffs, known to geologists as "talus slopes." The walls of Cataract, a superb gorge about forty miles long with a depth of 2,700 feet, are often nearly vertical. The rapids here are many and violent, the total fall being about 450 feet.

The Colorado River cuts through the Colorado Plateau to form this and subsequent canyons. The Paradox Formation, deposited 320 million years ago, is the oldest rock layer visible in Cataract Canyon. From the turbulent rapids, the river slows as it enters Glen Canyon, where it spreads out into a man-made feature formed less than sixty years ago, Lake Powell. Glen Canyon's sandstone walls are sometimes perpendicular to the lake for 1,000 feet, the highest walls being about 1,600 feet from the water. Meanwhile, other rivers, with their sources high in the mountains of southwest Colorado, have been merging together and heading for their fusion with the Colorado. Three of those rivers meet at yet another river town, Farmington, New Mexico.

A thrill ride through Cataract Canyon, Canyonlands National Park.

Farmington and Its Three Rivers

Farmington, New Mexico, is a quintessential river town. Three good-sized rivers join there—the Animas, La Plata, and the San Juan. Because of the abundant flowing water, there are several prehistoric ruins in the area, including Aztec and Salmon ruins, home of the Ancestral Pueblo people as early as AD 900.

ABOVE~Incised meanders of the San Juan River, Goosenecks State Park, Utah.

BELOW~The world's largest natural bridge, Rainbow Bridge has a 275-foot span and is 290 feet high. Rainbow Bridge National Monument, Utah.

Farmington's "Step Out" parks and walking trails program encourages people to walk for health, using the river park trails. The Berg/Animas Trail was added to the National Recreation Trails system in 2011. The four-mile network of trails along the Animas River winds through groves of native cottonwoods, runs along the river's edge, and crosses the river twice via bridges.

The trails also provide places to get onto the river by canoe, kayak, or raft. The river trail system includes an interactive water feature in Berg Park and the constructed white water rapids in Animas Park. The rapids, still a work in progress at the time of this writing, use strategically placed rocks at a certain point in the river to create the rapids, like the rapids at Glenwood Springs, Colorado.

After flowing through Farmington, the San Juan River, one of the major Colorado River tributaries, joins the big red river at Lake Powell. Most of the San Juan River flows through the Four Corners area where the four states come together, and it runs just a few miles northeast of the exact point where the four state boundaries meet.

Similar to the waters below Flaming Gorge Dam, there's a terrific fishing site in Navajo Lake State Park, extending four miles below Navajo Dam in northwest New Mexico, near Farmington. Some consider it one of the most revered trout fishing locations in North America. Known as the "Miracle Mile," the water here is cold and clear after its release from the Navajo Dam. The river flows smoothly and consistently, perfect for plant growth, which provides a habitat for insect growth, which in turn provides food for trout, and the trout's waste fertilizes the plant life in a natural symbiotic cycle.

The San Juan in Utah is also a popular river destination for kayaking and rapid running before it empties out into the calm waters of Lake Powell.

Lake Powell and the Glen Canyon Recreation Area

First there was a river, then there was a canyon, then there was a dam, and, finally, there was Lake Powell. In 1956, President Dwight D. Eisenhower pressed a button on his desk in the Oval Office at the White House, triggering the first demolition blast to reroute the flow of the Colorado River so the building of Glen Canyon Dam could begin. Three years later, the U.S. Bureau of Reclamation completed a bridge that rose 700 feet (210 m) above the river. Used for transportation of workers, equipment, and supplies, it was the world's highest arch bridge at the time. The town of Page, Arizona, was created to facilitate construction in the remote location.

ABOVE~A sand and cobble peninsula on Romana Mesa near Gunsight Butte, which overlooks Padre Bay, Lake Powell, in the Glen Canyon National Recreation Area, Utah.

BELOW~A view from the precipice: Horseshoe Bend, just south of Page, Arizona.

Completed in 1963, engineers used more than five million cubic yards of concrete in the 710-foot-high (216 m) dam's construction. The First Lady, Lady Bird Johnson, dedicated Glen Canyon Dam on Thursday, September 22, 1964. Hydroelectric turbines and generators were installed by 1966, supplying electric power to more than five million customers in Arizona, Colorado, Utah, New Mexico, Nevada, Nebraska, and Wyoming.

About two million people visit Lake Powell every year. Next to Lake Mead, it is the second-largest man-made reservoir in the United States. The 186-mile lake features ninety-six major side canyons. The shoreline is a phenomenal 1,960 miles long, whereas the combined shoreline of Washington, Oregon, and California is 1,293 miles!

ABOVE~Light shafts briefly penetrate Upper Antelope Canyon, near Page, Arizona.

BELOW~Mesas, clouds, and water: Lake Powell in layers.

The Glen Canyon National Recreation Area was created by an act of Congress on October 27, 1972, available to the public for camping, hiking, fishing, waterskiing, and jet skiing. Renting a houseboat is the most popular form of vacation lodging.

Because of its out-of-this-world sandstone formations, more than forty-five movies and television series have chosen Lake Powell as their shooting location, including the original Planet of the Apes (1968), producer/director Tim Burton's 2001 remake of *Planet of the Apes*, the award-winning *Gravity* (2013), and several episodes of the popular British science fiction series, *Doctor Who.*

From movies to houseboats, the majority of Glen Canyon National Recreation Area is in Utah, but the Colorado River continues south on past the dam into Arizona. There we find another one of those rare geographical opportunities to cross the river, this time at Lees Ferry.

Crossing at Lees Ferry

Lees Ferry, the most important landing on the Colorado River, is located nine miles south of the Utah/Arizona border where the Paria River (originally Pahreah, from a Paiute word meaning salty or muddy water), empties into the Colorado from the northwest. By the time it crosses from Utah into Arizona, the Colorado River is strong, fast, and dangerous. Over eons, rushing water, with its cargo of sand, gravel, and rocks, cut deep canyon channels for hundreds of miles. But around Lees Ferry, a valley was formed by a swell in the Colorado Plateau. The area contains sandstone, siltstone, shale, and limestone formed by ancient ocean sedimentation and the alluvial deposits from the Colorado and Paria.

These softer stones erode more easily than the rock layers upstream and down, so the Colorado slopes gently down to the river through a series of flat benchlands on either side of Lees Ferry. Because of this, Lees Ferry is the only place in 260 miles (418 km) where it is possible to cross by ferry and wagon.

Mormon pioneer John D. Lee started a ferry service there in 1873 to bring Mormon settlers into Arizona. Near the ferry, which occupied both sides of the Colorado, Lee home-steaded a ranch on the west bank of Paria Canyon, and put in a large farm and orchard, complete with a large irri-gation system. The place became known as Lonely Dell because of its location and greenery.

A tall steel automobile bridge was constructed across the river five miles south of Lees Ferry in 1929, but the ferry service operated for more than half a century before it became obsolete. Lees Ferry is still a major staging area for rafters and boaters entering the river to go through the Grand Canyon, where in just a few miles west of Lees Ferry, the river plunges down between the walls of a marble gorge created by the rapid rise of the Colorado Plateau on each side.

ABOVE~Lees Ferry is the most accessible river landing for trips into the Grand Canyon.

BELOW~The Grand Falls of the Little Colorado River, just east of Flagstaff, Arizona, flows like chocolate milk after a heavy rainstorm.

The Little Colorado River and Its Falls

The Little Colorado River begins in east-central Arizona's White Moun-tains, near Mount Baldy, at almost 10,000 feet, forty miles west of the New Mexico border. It runs almost 340 miles from there to its confluence with the Colorado near Cameron, Arizona. Only the beginning and end sections of the river run with any regularity all year long. Most of the time, the Little Colorado "river" is a wide, dry wash until there is a heavy rain or snowmelt. Nor-mally, the river is colored bright blue by dissolved travertine and limestone, just like Havasu Creek at the west end of the Grand Canyon.

The Little Colorado River joins the Colorado River near Desert View, in Grand Canyon National Park, and for its last forty miles it runs through a canyon deep enough to be called a gorge. Here, the "Colorado Chiquito" (Little Colorado) carves the narrow, 3,200-foot (980 m) deep Little Colorado River Gorge into the Colorado Plateau. The best view of this is about ten miles west of Cameron, Arizona, on Highway 64, one of the main roads leading to the Grand Canyon. There is a parking lot at this spot, and more than a dozen Navajo families sell their arts and crafts there.

This breathtaking view is not for the timid or, for that matter, for the overly bold. There is very little in the way of restraints at the edge of the gorge, so you may want to keep a firm grip on any children you would like to keep.

The Little Colorado continues its flow westward until just east of Flagstaff, Arizona, where you may see a large waterfall. It happens during spring snowmelts, usually in March or April. Then, if there is enough water, the river falls 185 feet (56 m) over the Grand Falls of the Little Colorado, affectionately called "Chocolate Falls" because its thick, muddy color looks like milk chocolate. It is surprising to consider that the famous Niagara Falls drops only 167 feet, but the Grand Falls is taller. However, it is a series of several steps, and usually has water in it only a few weeks every year.

John Wesley Powell

John Wesley Powell, Civil War hero, geology professor, naturalist, and ethnographer, was the first man that we know of to take an expedition through the Grand Canyon via the Green and Colorado rivers, and his subsequent publications put the canyon on the map, both literally and figuratively.

A noon day rest in Marble Canyon on Powell's 1872 expedition.

Powell wrote a detailed report of his river expeditions, and also wrote a series of articles for *Scribner's Magazine*, presenting the most detailed and beautiful descriptions of the cliffs, canyons, and rapids.

He designed four 21-foot rowboats with three compartments. With enough provisions to last ten men ten months, they set off from Green River, Wyoming, on May 24, 1869. Just a few days later, in the Canyon of Lodore, they lost one of the boats and most of their scientific survey instruments with it.

Reaching the Grand Canyon on August 29th, Powell abandoned another boat and a large number of instruments, believing what lay ahead would be too much for them. The remaining crew ran the river the next day and disembarked at the mouth of the Virgin River, near present-day Las Vegas, Nevada.

Because they did not have all their instruments the first time, a second trip was needed to complete the survey of the rivers and canyons. On May 22nd, 1871, Powell's second expedition left Green River and reached the mouth of the Kanab Wash by September of 1872, but high water kept them from running the last 125 miles.

Powell was appointed as the second director of the U.S. Geological Survey and served from 1881–1894. He also served as the director for the Smithsonian Institution's Bureau of Ethnology until his death in 1902.

Chapter 3

Through, Around, and Above the Grand Canyon

The Grandest Canyon in the World?

Like the confluences of the Yampa and Green, or Green and Colorado, the most tempestuous stretches of a river follow the clash of two powerful water forces.

Frederick Dellenbaugh called the Grand Canyon "the longest, deepest, and most difficult of any canyon in the world." We now know that there are deeper canyons; nonetheless, it still deserves the name "Grand." But it was not always known by that name.

Marble Canyon

South of Lees Ferry, the Colorado River flows into Marble Canyon, under Navajo Bridge. Traditionally, the beginning of Grand Canyon was considered to be the confluence of the Little Colorado and Colorado rivers. But in 1975, Marble Canyon National Monument became part of Grand Canyon National Park.

Like many place names all over the world, the name of this canyon is misleading. There is no marble in Marble Canyon. Major John Wesley Powell, a geology professor at Illinois Wesleyan University at the time of

OPPOSITE~From Lees Ferry to this view looking west from Navajo Bridge, the walls of Marble Canyon loom above the Colorado River.

RIGHT~Old Navajo Bridge is now a pedestrian bridge offering excellent views of the Colorado River below, and sometimes you can see California condors soaring underneath.

the expedition, knew that it was not marble. But he said, "The limestone of the canyon is often polished, and it makes a beautiful marble. Sometimes the rocks are of many colors—white, gray, pink, and purple, with saffron tints." It was phrases like this, from Powell's *Scribner's Monthly* article, that made people fall in love with the Grand Canyon before they even saw it.

ABOVE~Sandstone formations look as though they've been designed by Salvador Dali at "The Wave" by North Coyote Buttes. On the Utah/Arizona border, west of Lake Powell.

LEFT~Backpackers in Paria Canyon, Vermilion Cliffs Wilderness Area, Utah.

Return of the California Condors

Condors have hard scales on their feet that, when seen up close, seem to scream out 'we stem from an ancient line of reptiles!'

—Phil McKenna,
"Unearthing How Dinosaurs Became Birds,"
www.audubonsociety.org

About thirty miles north of the Grand Canyon, Vermilion Cliffs National Monument is home to an outstanding California condor breeding and reintroduction program. Condors have been released every year since 1996, and each bird is fitted with a radio transmitter that biologists monitor daily.

The largest flying land bird in North America, California condors have a wingspan of up to nine and a half feet, can soar more than fifty miles per hour, and can travel one hundred miles in one day. Some condors live to be sixty years old in the wild, mate for life, and females lay a single egg annually or every other year.

According to Arizona Game and Fish officials, male and female condors are identical in size and plumage. The juveniles, however, have dark-colored heads until they are about four years old, and their bill color changes from black to ivory as they mature.

Ancestral condor fossils date back more than 35 million years, when their habitat ranged from Mexico to Canada, across the southern United States from California to Florida, and as far north as New York. Prehistoric condor feathers, bones, and even eggshells have been found in remote Grand Canyon caves.

The condors' range contracted considerably when vast numbers of their prey—saber-toothed cats, mastodons, and giant sloths—died out during the Pleistocene epoch about 10,000 years ago. But the giant birds survived on the Pacific coast from Baja, California, to British Columbia, probably feeding on large sea mammals that washed up on the shore.

The population declined rapidly from the 1880s to the 1930s because of shooting, poisoning, power line collisions, and reduction of wilderness habitat. The last condor sighting in Arizona was in 1924; from then on, only those in California remained.

The California condor was placed on the endangered species list in 1967. The population dropped to an all time low of twenty-two birds in 1982, and a captive breeding program began in 1983. Arizona followed with a similar program in 1996.

But in 1985, only nine birds remained in the wild, according to National Park Service staff. This prompted a controversial decision to capture the remaining condors and make them part of the breeding program.

Ornithologists now remove each condor egg as soon as it is laid and place it in an incubator, which usually prompts the mother to produce a second, and sometimes third egg, thus speeding up the process. By 2005, there were 270 condors, and the world population increased to a phenomenal 425 condors by 2014.

How the Grand Canyon Was Formed

From Hermit Rim the river writhes like a snake that,
raging desperately against the steady up-push of the land,
has stuck its fangs into its own side.

　　　—MARY AUSTIN, *The Land of Journey's Ending,* 1920

This view from Pima Point shows
the grandeur so hard to capture in
photographs.

Earth, wind, water, and fire: Nature used every tool in its kit to form
the Grand Canyon—faulting, uplifting, volcanism, weathering, erosion,
and sedimentation. Here's a simple review of how they operate. Faults
are cracks in the earth's surface where a rock formation breaks into
pieces that then move in different directions from each other. Uplift
is caused by faulting, but instead of tilting, a block of rock and soil is
raised vertically several thousand feet while remaining horizontal, forming a plateau. Volcanism occurs when hot liquid magma and gases from
inside the earth burst through openings in the earth's crust. The magma
erupts as molten lava and ash, which cool and harden into igneous rock.
Weathering is the decomposition of rocks, soils, and minerals by heat,
air, water, and pressure. Erosion is similar, but involves breakdown and
transport of rocks by wind and water and the suspended or dissolved
particles they carry with them. These particles eventually settle on the
earth's surface or on the bottom of lakes and oceans. There they harden
into flat-layered rock formations by the process called sedimentation.
Volcanoes and faults are usually caused by a larger global process that
geologists call plate tectonics.

ABOVE~Point Imperial, on the north rim of the Grand Canyon, provides a glimpse that most visitors never see.

BELOW~A glowing view of Marble Canyon, prelude to the Grand Canyon.

OVERLEAF~It is hard to believe that a meandering river created this stunning vista of the Grand Canyon and the Bright Angel Trail.

In 1912, Alfred Wegener expanded on centuries-old observations that the coastlines of South America and Africa fit closely together like pieces of a giant jigsaw puzzle and that all continents were probably once joined together in one big landmass, which he called Pangaea.

Modifications to Wegener's original ideas explained how earth's rocky crust broke into pieces called tectonic plates and floated around on the hotter, more fluid upper mantle below the plates. The plates continue to bump into each other and pull away, causing earthquakes, volcanic activity, and uplifts that raise ocean floors thousands of feet, turning them into plateaus and mountains where the plates collide, and in some unusual cases, such as the Laramide orogeny, even far from where the tectonic plates overlap.

Arizona's geology is a process of pulling apart and pushing together over 4.5 billion years. The rock layers' different hardnesses and resistance to weathering and erosion created the cliffs and ledges of the Grand Canyon.

The Vishnu Schist at the bottom of the Grand Canyon was laid down as sediment approximately 1.74 billion years ago. About 300 million years later, collisional forces lifted the rock into a mountain range as high as the Himalayas. These mountains eroded into a flat plane over tens of millions of years. A second mountain range was raised about a billion years ago, and that was also reduced, by erosion over millions of years, to a flat surface.

Later, the whole area was alternately submerged under inland seas or raised above the water to form beaches and sand dunes. Deposited sediments hardened into shale, sandstone, and limestone, trapping and fossilizing sea plants and animals in the process. About six million years ago, the region uplifted as the Colorado Plateau, and the Colorado River cut through the many rock formations as it rose. It would be a long time before humans would live in the Canyon, though.

Tusayan Pueblo

The Tusayan ruin, about three miles west of the Desert View Watchtower on the South Rim of the Grand Canyon, gives a fairly good overview of the peoples who lived in the Grand Canyon area during Ancestral Puebloan times. As much as 10,000 years ago, nomadic Paleo-Indian hunter/gatherers hunted now-extinct ice-age mammals in the Grand Canyon region.

According to dendrochronological dating (dendrochronology works by matching the growth patterns of tree-ring samples of unknown date to tree-ring chronologies of known date from the same area) the Ancestral Pueblo people built this small U-shaped pueblo around AD 1185. There is a small museum near the pueblo, displaying some of the artifacts uncovered during excavation of the site in the 1930s. The museum also exhibits small split-willow figures of deer and mountain sheep, which the Archaic People created and kept in canyon caves 2,000 to 4,000 years ago.

This split-twig figure was made between two thousand and four thousand years ago by a member of the Archaic culture.

How the Grand Canyon Became Grand

Ours has been the first, and will doubtless be the last party of whites to visit this profitless locality…It seems intended by nature that the Colorado, along the greater part of its lonely and majestic way, shall be forever unvisited and undisturbed.

—LIEUTENANT JOSEPH CHRISTMAS IVES, 1858

The Grand Canyon was not always so famous. In previous centuries, when nature was something to be feared and conquered, the formidable canyon was viewed with awe, but considered more a foe than a natural wonder.

In September 1540, Spanish conquistador Francisco Vasquez de Coronado sent Captain Garcia López de Cárdenas and twelve soldiers west from the Pueblo Indian villages near present-day Albuquerque to search for a large river north of the Hopi mesas.

Led by Hopi guides, they probably reached the South Rim, between today's Desert View and Moran Point. Cárdenas estimated that the canyon was about eight to ten miles wide, which it is at that point. However, they thought the river was only about six feet wide, but it was actually three hundred. Desperate for water, they searched for four days to find a way down and finally sent three agile men into the canyon. Although Cárdenas admitted that the sights were spectacular, he reported to Francisco Coronado that the way was impassable.

It was Major John Wesley Powell (left) who put the Grand Canyon on the map. In 1915, a National Academy of Science biography credited Powell with creating national interest in the Grand Canyon. "His famous volume, *Exploration of the Colorado River of the West*, [is] one of the best narratives of adventure anywhere to be found," said the Academy.

Even though Powell reached more than 5,000 American readers with his words, the artist Thomas Moran, invited by Powell to accompany him on his second expedition of the canyon in 1872, painted "Chasm of the Colorado," which was worth more than a thousand words. The U.S. Congress purchased the huge painting and displayed it in the Capitol Building in Washington, D.C.

The Atchison, Topeka and Santa Fe Railway purchased the rights to reproduce Moran's "Chasm of the Colorado" and used it as the company's calendar for many years, perfecting the public image of America's grandest canyon.

The Desert View Watchtower, built in 1932, was modeled after prehistoric towers. The observation platform offers the most expansive views of the Grand Canyon landscape.

Desert View Watchtower

Twenty-five miles east of the Grand Canyon Visitor Center stands an impressive 70-foot (21 m) five-story tower made of large rocks built on an interior steel-beam framework. Completed in 1932, it is also known as the Indian Watchtower because Fred Harvey Company architect Mary Jane Elizabeth Colter researched and visited ancient Ancestral Pueblo structures in Arizona, Colorado, and New Mexico to create a design that was evocative of American Indian tradition. And the Watchtower itself serves as a sort of "gateway" to tribal lands east of the National Park.

Narrow stairways against the interior walls take you to the observation deck at the top. From there you can see the Colorado River far below, and vistas reach dozens of miles in every direction.

World-renowned Hopi Indian artist Fred Kabotie painted the murals that decorate the inside walls of the Hopi room (second floor). He and Fred Geary painted other murals in the tower. Desert View Watchtower and overlook provide exceptionally good views of the Colorado River, eastern Grand Canyon, the Vermilion Cliffs, and Navajo Mountain. A trading post and concession stand with picnic tables are located nearby.

Phantom Ranch

Built in 1922, this historic lodge designed by Mary Colter is located adjacent to Bright Angel Creek near the Colorado River. Bright Angel Pueblo, an Ancestral Puebloan site dating to between late 1000 and 1150 CE, is within walking distance of Phantom Ranch Lodge. You can only reach the ranch by mule, on foot, or by a multiple-day rafting trip on the Colorado River. Colter called this collection of rustic cabins and a main lodge "Phantom Ranch" after nearby Phantom Creek. The ranch is built of native stone and wood to blend in with the natural surroundings. Phantom Ranch is the only public lodging in the inner canyon. It is a remote but picturesque place to sit quietly by the banks of Bright Angel Creek or the mighty Colorado River.

The Kolb Brothers Make a Movie

You really can't talk about the Grand Canyon without mentioning the Kolb brothers, Ellsworth and Emery. Older brother Ellsworth, born in Pittsburgh, went to work as a bellboy at the Bright Angel Hotel in 1901, and his brother Emery followed a year later.

They purchased a photography business in Williams, Arizona, sixty miles south of the Grand Canyon, and carved out a shelf on the canyon's rim at the beginning of Bright Angel Trail. They took pictures of tourists riding mules into the canyon in the morning, and had the finished prints ready for them when the saddle-sore tourists returned in the afternoon.

In 1911, they retraced John Wesley Powell's 1869 trip, starting from Green River, Wyoming. Even better, they captured it on film, a relatively new process at the time. That movie was shown in their Grand Canyon studio from 1915 until Emery Kolb's death in 1976, sixty years without missing a day. That makes it the longest continuously shown film in the world.

OPPOSITE~The view from Toroweap is the steepest drop directly to the river.

BELOW~Visible proof that Lava Falls is one of the most exciting rapids in the Grand Canyon.

Lava Falls Rapids

I do not know much about gods; but I think that the river
Is a strong brown god—sullen, untamed and intractable,
Patient to some degree, at first recognised as a frontier;
Useful, untrustworthy, as a conveyor of commerce;
Then only a problem confronting the builder of bridges.
The problem once solved, the brown god is almost forgotten
By the dwellers in cities—ever, however, implacable.

—T. S. ELIOT, *Four Quartets: The Dry Salvages*, 1941

Lava Falls is known as one of the most exciting and challenging of the Grand Canyon rapids. Named for nearby lava flows that created dark basalt formations on the north side of the Colorado River, it is located at Mile 179 along the Colorado River within Grand Canyon National Park, with Lees Ferry being Mile 0.0 at the east end. Millions of years ago, cooling lava created a rock dam more than two thousand feet high, which created a lake stretching from this point all the way back to Moab, Utah. The dam broke apart long ago, but the river drops thirteen feet at this point, "the scariest ten seconds of the river," as one boater put it.

Toroweap or Tuweep; Which Is It?

Actually, it's both, depending on how you use the terms. The two words are both Paiute and are often interchangeable. Tuweep means "the Earth." It's the name of an early Mormon settlement and also the National Park Service's term for the whole area. On the other hand, Toroweap means "dry or barren valley," and is used to refer to the overlook and specific valley.

Toroweap Overlook is on the North Rim fifty-five miles from the North Rim Headquarters as the crow flies, but 148 miles by a remote, winding road. The canyon wall drops 3,000 feet (880 m) straight down

from the overlook, making it one of the most dramatic views in the National Park from the rim to the Colorado River. As a result, intrepid professional photographers are willing to endure the drive to "get the shot."

Havasu Falls

The Havasupai people, or Havasuw `Baaja, "people of the blue green waters," take their name after the most beautiful waterfalls in the Grand Canyon area. Many Havasupai people live near the idyllic falls in Supai Village. The village is supposed to be the only one in the United States where mail is still delivered by mule.

The Havasupai are Yuman-speakers. Some archaeologists consider them descendants of the prehistoric Cerbat peoples of the lower Colorado River. They have no migration story because they have lived in these lush and remote canyons along Havasu Creek since the beginning of time, and consider themselves the guardians of the Grand Canyon.

What makes the water so blue? Havasu Creek's vibrant sky-blue and turquoise water coloration is created when the water seeps or bubbles through the unique limestone layer in that area and absorbs high concentrations of carbon dioxide. This dissolves the carbonate rocks in the groundwater. When the water is no longer under pressure, the calcium carbonate separates and forms columns and horizontal slabs, or benches, of a mineral called travertine. These solids form dams in the streams, and when these fill up, they spill over into waterfalls. Floods sometimes destroy these dams, and with them the waterfalls, but new ones are forming constantly.

Havasu Falls is the most visited of the various falls along Havasu Creek. Here, the main stream flows over a sheer cliff and drops more than ninety feet (27 m) into a large pool below. Access is limited to hiking and helicopter, but even so it is still quite popular. Just outside the border of Grand Canyon National Park, another tribe has created one of the world's most unusual tourist attractions, the Skywalk, and it is quite a bit easier to reach.

OPPOSITE~Havasu means "blue water" in the Havasupai language, and Havasu Falls live up to the name.

BELOW~The Skywalk is one of the best man-made viewpoints in the world.

The Hualapai Tribe and Their Skywalk

Hualapai means "People of the Pines," and they are descendants of the prehistoric peoples of the western end of the Grand Canyon. The Sky-

walk is a phenomenal piece of architectural engineering, the only structure of its kind in the world. It is a horseshoe-shaped steel frame covered with five layers of thick glass, completed in 2007 at a cost of about $30 million.

The platform juts out about seventy feet (21 m) from the rim of the Grand Canyon, giving observers the highest view possible down to the river at the bottom of the canyon of more than 4,000 feet (1,219 m). In comparison, the world's tallest building, the Burj Khalifa, is 2,717 feet tall (829 m).

West of the Skywalk on the Colorado River is another huge engineering phenomenon, and this one helped create a city in the desert that receives more than 41 million visitors per year—Las Vegas, Nevada. But first, some background on how all this water that has tumbled, roared, and rolled for more than two thousand miles by this point came to be tamed, and how the Colorado River water is divided up among the states.

Refilling the Salton Sea

By the early 1900s, farmers all along the Colorado River south of the Grand Canyon began building canals to divert the waters to irrigate their crops. But the wild and unpredictable river wiped out many efforts. In his 1911 novel, *The Winning of Barbara Worth*, Harold Bell Wright describes the biggest water control failure, in which the Colorado River jumped its banks and ran west instead of south for almost a hundred miles and refilled the ancient Salton Sea, 234 feet (71.3 m) below sea level.

In 1905, engineers from the California Development Company dug irrigation canals and cut into the riverbank to avoid silt build-up. The grade from the river into the canals was steeper than its natural course, so the river followed gravity into the easier course. This was during a high flood year, and the huge overflow rushed into the canal, diverting the Colorado River from its bed. The engineers underestimated the water's force, and the wooden headings, spillways, and gates were not strong enough to hold back the river.

The water overflowed the irrigation channel and followed old desert washes. Farmers evacuated, building levees around towns and then fleeing as the water overwhelmed them. One channel grew bigger and the current got stronger. Then the Colorado River began cutting a vertical waterfall a quarter of a mile wide and eighty feet tall. The renegade river flowed on this new path for two years before the breach could be plugged. Eventually, a railroad track was constructed near the gap, and a large wooden trestle was built across the roaring channel. Tons of rocks were brought in by railroad cars to fill the channel.

Historians believe that this disaster partially led to the movement to build dams to better control the Colorado River.

ABOVE~Redwall Cavern, Marble Canyon, Grand Canyon National Park, Arizona.

LEFT~ River-running pioneer and conservationist Martin Litton rowing Lava Falls at the age of eighty-seven.

Colorado River Compact

As Major John Wesley Powell predicted in his *Report on the Lands of the Arid Region* in 1878, the dry West could not be settled like the much wetter East, and would require serious planning to provide water for settlers homesteading and farming the West, and the many generations that would follow.

By 1922, it was obvious to representatives of the seven states watered by the Colorado River that Powell was right. Representatives from the

Prehistoric granaries in the Marble Canyon cliff walls near Nankoweap were built by Ancestral Puebloans.

seven concerned states got together at Bishop's Lodge, near Santa Fe, New Mexico, and created the Colorado River Compact, an agreement governing allocations of water rights in the vast Colorado River Basin.

They divided the Colorado River drainage into upper and lower basins—Wyoming, Colorado, Utah, and New Mexico for the upper, and Nevada, Arizona, and California for the lower—with the dividing point at Lees Ferry. According to the compact, the Upper Basin states were not to take more than 7,500,000-acre-feet (30,000 km²) during any ten-year period. (An acre-foot is 325,851 gallons, the amount it takes to cover an acre of land one foot deep in water.) Going by rainfall patterns in the years previous to the signing, this was estimated to be an equal portion for both basins. However, tree-ring studies indicate that the annual flow of the Colorado River, instead of the 16,400,000-acre-feet predicted, was usually two to three million acre-feet less. This created the problem of dividing up water that didn't exist in the first place.

The Colorado Compact allowed for the irrigation of western farmlands, and the eventual construction of Hoover Dam and Lake Powell, along with other federal and state water projects along the Colorado River administered by the United States Bureau of Reclamation.

Arizona's Governor George W. P. Hunt opposed the compact and refused to sign it, claiming that it gave too much water to California. Governor Hunt was Arizona's first governor when statehood arrived in 1912, and was elected governor seven times, finishing in 1932. His opposition to the compact became a major plank in his political campaigns, to the point that political correspondents quipped that, "While Jesus had walked on water, their governor ran on the Colorado."

4

Desert Dams and Cities

As railroads began to reach remote parts of the Southwest, making it easier for homesteading farmers to reach the arid lands, they soon realized what John Wesley Powell meant about the necessity to irrigate. But it was not easy to harness a powerful river like the Colorado.

Previous attempts to control the river indicated that it would take something on a grand scale, an undertaking so massive that no local groups could afford it, to get water from the river to their fields through safe, reliable methods. Westerners took their concerns to Washington D.C., and in 1902, Congress passed the Lowlands Reclamation Act, also known as the Newlands Act after Nevada Representative Francis Newlands, who introduced the bill. President Theodore Roosevelt created legislative alliances to assure the bill's passage. The Newlands Act gave the secretary of the interior authority to determine reclamation projects in twenty states and territories, primarily to create dams to provide water to the public for agricultural purposes.

Once the Colorado River Compact decided how much water would go to the Lower Basin, it was then necessary to develop a means to deliver that water. The dam's purpose was threefold: provide flood control, irrigation water, and hydroelectric power.

By the turn of the century, engineers knew that Boulder Canyon, or nearby Black Canyon, would be a good spot to build a dam. What they needed was a fairly narrow canyon with high walls of hard rock to wedge the giant concrete wall into. The second important factor is a large water source, and in the West, sources don't come any bigger than the Colorado River.

The Boulder Canyon Project (eventually known as Hoover Dam), first presented to Congress in 1922, was approved in 1928. Construction began in 1931, during the depths of the Great Depression. President Franklin D. Roosevelt dedicated the dam on September 30, 1935, and the construction companies finished their work in 1936, two years ahead of schedule.

We recognize also the energy, resourcefulness and zeal of the
builders, who, under the greatest physical obstacles, have pushed
this work forward to completion two years in advance of the contract
requirements. But especially, we express our gratitude to the
thousands of workers who gave brain and brawn to this great work
of construction.

—PRESIDENT FRANKLIN D. ROOSEVELT,
Boulder Dam dedication, 1935

Construction of the dam employed thousands of workers, more than
one hundred of whom were killed during the dangerous enterprise.

Hoover Dam, 726.4 feet high, 1,244 feet wide, 660 feet thick at the
bottom, and 45 feet thick at the top, was the largest dam in the world at
the time of its completion. It took 3,250,000 cubic yards of concrete to
complete Hoover Dam, plus another 1,500,000 cubic yards for supporting structures. It was, and still is, a true marvel of modern engineering.
According to President Roosevelt, "The price of Boulder Dam during the
depression years provided [work] for 4,000 men, most of them heads of
families, and many thousands more were enabled to earn a livelihood
through manufacture of materials and machinery."

Power generated by the dam serves public and private utilities in Arizona, California, and Nevada, and nearly a million people tour the dam
each year. In October 2010, the Hoover Dam Bypass opened, moving
traffic away from driving directly on top of the dam.

Remote Gregg Basin on Lake Mead
is perfect for fishing, camping, and
waterskiing.

Lake Mead National Recreation Area

The water impounded behind Hoover Dam created Lake Mead, named
for Bureau of Reclamation Commissioner Elwood Mead. At its maximum
capacity, it is the largest reservoir in the United States. Spanning the
Arizona/Nevada border, Lake Mead is 112 miles (180 km) long and has
759 miles of shoreline when full. However, due to water demands and
prolonged drought, the lake has not been full for more than thirty years.

Boulder, then Hoover, then Boulder, and Finally Hoover

The first major dam on the Colorado after it joined with the Green River was supposed to be built in Boulder Canyon, about thirty miles southeast of Las Vegas, and so the Bureau of Reclamation initiated the Boulder Canyon Project to build it there. Then the engineers found that nearby Black Canyon, several miles downstream, was a better location, but it was still referred to as Boulder Dam because the government legislative process had already been started. It would be difficult to change names in midstream (midriver in this case) without a lot more red tape and confusion.

The intake towers on the upstream side of Hoover Dam direct water into the penstocks (floodgates that control water flow).

And then the naming process became personal and political. After running for President in 1920 and then supporting Republican candidate Warren G. Harding, California engineer Herbert Hoover was appointed Secretary of Commerce when Harding was elected. As such, Hoover played a leadership role in the Colorado River Compact and spearheaded federal support for the Boulder Dam Project. Because of these efforts, when the dam was dedicated on September 17th, 1930, Secretary of the Interior Ray Wilbur announced, "I have the honor and privilege of giving a name to this new structure. In Black Canyon, under the Boulder Canyon Project Act, it shall be called Hoover Dam."

This was not surprising, because by this time Hoover was the U.S. President, and therefore he was Ray Wilbur's boss. But Wilbur also pointed out that Hoover was "the great engineer whose vision and persistence, first as chairman of the Colorado River Commission in 1922, and on so many other occasions since, has done so much to make the dam possible." However, many Americans felt that President Hoover was responsible for the Great Depression and did not appreciate having his name associated with any project that would put him in a positive light. To add to the confusion, the press continued to use both names, although it was always referred to as Hoover Dam in official documents.

But then Democrat Franklin Delano Roosevelt carried 42 of the 48 states in the 1932 election, and President Hoover left the White House after only one term in office. President Roosevelt replaced Secretary of Commerce Wilbur with Harold Ickes, a Progressive Republican. Soon after his appointment, Ickes changed the name back to Boulder Dam, stating, "The men who pioneered this project knew it by this name."

However, in 1947, when President Harry Truman was in the White House, the 80th Congress passed Resolution 140, restoring the name Hoover Dam permanently. The resolution stated that "as President, Herbert Hoover took an active part in settling the engineering problems and location of the dam in Black Canyon. . .the construction contracts were signed under his administration, and when he left office construction had been pushed to a point where it was more than a year ahead of schedule."

The lake is administered by the National Park Service, and the location was renamed the Lake Mead National Recreation Area in 1964, adding the Shivwits Plateau and Lake Mohave to the area, offering recreation options all year round. Lake Mead National Recreation Area parallels the course of the Colorado River as it flows west out of the Grand Canyon and hooks abruptly south toward the Gulf of California. The Recreation Area is at the crossroads of three of North America's four great deserts: the Sonoran, the Mojave, and the Great Basin, and the park's ecosystem is made up of plants and animals from all of them.

Like most other locations in the Lower Colorado River Basin, boating is the most popular activity here, from motorized craft to canoeing and kayaking. Similar to Utah and Colorado, back-road bicycling is rapidly gaining interest as well. Other sports that bring people to the area include fishing, swimming, and waterskiing. Lake Mead has four marinas and many secluded coves with sandy beaches nestled in among the rocky cliffs.

The Mike O'Callaghan–Pat Tillman Memorial Bridge is an impressive complement to an already monumental man-made wonder, Hoover Dam.

The Mike O'Callaghan–Pat Tillman Memorial Bridge

The Hoover Dam did its job for almost eight decades, but eventually a bypass was needed to ease traffic conditions in the area. A key element to the Hoover Dam Bypass Project, the Mike O'Callaghan–Pat Tillman Memorial Bridge (opened in October, 2010) rerouted U.S. 93 traffic from its original route along the top of the dam and at the same time removed the previous highway's blind curves and hairpin turns. The bridge is named for former Nevada governor Mike O'Callaghan and Arizona Cardinals football player Pat Tillman. Tillman left his football career to join the United States Army after the September 11th, 2001, terrorist attacks. Tillman was killed in Afghanistan in 2004 at age 28. The bridge combines 16 million pounds of steel with 30,000 cubic yards of concrete, and is one of the widest twin-ribbed arch bridges in the Western Hemisphere.

Las Vegas, Nevada, Is No Longer a Meadow

While scouting the area for Mexican merchant Antonio Armijo in 1829 on their way from Santa Fe, New Mexico, to Los Angeles, California, Raphael Rivera named this area Las Vegas (the meadows) for good reason. In addition to being surrounded by mountains that provide runoff water, the natural artesian springs in the area created a green meadow surrounded by cottonwood and willow trees.

More than 12,000 years ago, the area around what is now Las Vegas, Nevada, was lush grassland where ancient peoples hunted prehistoric

camels and saber-toothed cats. Later, natives began growing crops, and eventually their descendants, the Paiute and Ute Indians, settled here.

John C. Fremont, who also led expeditions along the Green River in Wyoming with Kit Carson, described Las Vegas in a report and put it on a map in 1845. After a false start in 1855, Mormon settlers returned to the area in 1867 and settled permanently.

A few ranchers and prospectors worked the area, but it wasn't until the San Pedro, Los Angeles, and Salt Lake Railroad arrived in 1905 that a town began to grow. The town incorporated in 1911. Nevada outlawed gambling in 1910, but speakeasies and illegal casinos survived until Nevada legalized gambling again in 1931.

Being only thirty miles away to the northwest of the proposed dam site, Las Vegas residents wanted their town to be construction headquarters for the Boulder Dam Project, but those in charge created a new town for the headquarters.

The Bellagio and Luxor hotels are true oases on the great river, much like the pyramids on the Nile.

Six Companies, Inc., the six combined construction companies that won the bid to build the dam, created Boulder City, only seven miles from the Black Canyon dam site. At that time, Las Vegas's population was about 5,000 people, and soon there were almost 20,000 unemployed able-bodied workers flooding into the area from all over the United States.

Las Vegas bloomed after World War II, when a string of tourist hotels was built along a strip. In 1951, Frank Sinatra first performed in Las Vegas at the Desert Inn. He became a main attraction, and was joined in the early 1960s at the Sands Hotel by singer, actor, and comedian friends Dean Martin, Peter Lawford, Sammy Davis Jr., and Joey Bishop, the famous "Rat Pack."

Also in the 1960s, the man who Las Vegas reporters called the "bashful billionaire," recluse Howard Hughes, purchased the Desert Inn Hotel. According to local sources, he did more than anyone previously had to build hotel/casinos and create jobs.

By far the biggest Las Vegas attraction, however, was the "King of Rock and Roll," Elvis Presley. He didn't fare well the first time he played there in 1957, but by the time he returned in the early 1970s, Presley hit it big and signed a five-year contract to perform twice a year for four weeks for $125,000 per week. Elvis became Las Vegas's biggest icon, and is still a presence today.

Boulder City, the Dam Town

The six construction companies that won the bid to build the dam, appropriately named "Six Companies," were afraid that Las Vegas's rough and lawless Wild West atmosphere would not be conducive to keeping construction workers sharp on a dangerous job, and so a company town came into being overnight, like a mining town or a military post.

When the Boulder Canyon Project began in the summer of 1930, construction workers lived in tents and shacks near the banks of the Colorado River. Then, on a slight slope seven miles southwest of the project, federal and Six Companies employees began to build a town. By the end of 1931, what came to be called Boulder City had 2,500 residents. That number grew to more than 6,000 by 1934.

Because it was a federal reservation, no gambling, whiskey, or prostitution were tolerated. The city manager kept an eye on people's morals, and the rules were set down and strictly enforced by the Bureau of Reclamation construction engineer. Because everyone was employed, or related to someone who was, the quality of life was good compared to Depression-stricken America.

Like mining towns when the ore gives out, most construction towns turn into ghost towns, just a lot of empty buildings and full cemeteries. But when the federal government relinquished control of the town in 1959, locals created a government and kept raising their families there. Soon, more people moved in, some to work, some to retire. In 2009, *Money* magazine ranked Boulder City sixth in its list of the top twenty-five places to retire to in the United States based on affordable housing, medical care, tax rates, and arts and leisure.

As the Colorado River travels directly south from Las Vegas into the Mojave and Sonoran deserts, the residents of these river towns adapt to the climate. In contrast to the northern river areas, where some residents leave in the winter, here there are homes for winter residents, retirement havens, and plenty of boating and waterskiing. And the fishing is great; that's one thing that holds true the whole length of the Green and Colorado rivers.

The Arizona/California Border and Beyond

I wanted to be the first to view a country on which the eye of a white man had never gazed and to follow the course of rivers that run through a new land.
    —JEDEDIAH SMITH, 1820s fur trapper

From Las Vegas on down to Mexico, the Colorado River flows through three of the four great deserts in North America: The Great Basin, the Mojave, and the Sonoran. The fourth, the Chihuahuan, lies farther east in southern New Mexico and west Texas. Deserts are defined as areas that receive less than 10 inches (25 cm) of rain per year. And when it does rain, twenty percent of that amount can fall in one day, often violently. This sporadic heavy rainfall creates dry river beds called arroyos, or washes. These can become raging torrents during or immediately after a storm, causing a wall of water up to six feet high to flood through the desert channels in a matter of minutes, taking trees, small animals,

OPPOSITE~Lake Mohave, a reservoir formed by Davis Dam, has lost the muddy red color that gave it its name as a result of processing at Hoover Dam.

and even people with it. When these floods reach a mighty river, such as the River Nile in Egypt, the Yellow River in China, or the Colorado, the rivers swell into dangerous, uncontrollable waterways. But desert dwellers welcome the storms that bring life to the desert. In *The Colorado*, Frank Waters says this about watering holes in the desert:

> The paradox is the exotic lushness of their flowers. There are over seven hundred flowering plants in the desert, most of which have pushed their way north from the Sonoran Desert of Mexico. The right combination of weather and a bit of rain in the early spring brings them out overnight. For a week at best the desert is transformed into a brilliant garden of purple lupines, pink verbena, white primroses, mariposa lilies, and thousand-hued cactus flowers.

Laughlin: A New Town in the Old West

Unusual things grow in the desert, often in the most desolate places. The river can be a lifeline, making it possible to survive in extreme conditions. Botanists say that the desert has at least five seasons: fall, winter, spring, dry summer, and wet summer. Some plants don't grow every year but rather only when conditions are right. In that sense, they may be considered late bloomers, like the town of Laughlin, Nevada.

Located in the pointy southern tip of Nevada, Laughlin is an unincorporated town ninety miles south of Las Vegas. Like that city to its north, Laughlin is a gaming, headlining-entertainment, and water-recreation location. The population in 2010 was 7,323, but that number

ABOVE~Desert landscape of creosote, barrel cactus, and brittlebush where the Colorado River passes through Arizona, California, and Nevada.

BELOW~A male collared lizard basks in the sun.

Davis Dam with Laughlin, Nevada, in the background.

swells to more than four times that in the winter time with seasonal residents and tourists.

As the name indicates, the town is the dream of one man: Don Laughlin. A native of Owatonna, Minnesota, Laughlin bought the place formerly known as South Pointe (in the middle of the desert but nonetheless on the river), in 1964. There he opened the Riverside Resort on the west bank of the Colorado River. At this point, the elevation is a mere 570 feet above sea level. The river has dropped more than five thousand feet in about eight hundred miles from Glenwood Springs, Colorado.

Today, Laughlin is the third-most-visited resort and casino location in the state, and is one of the top five destination sites in the United States for RV (recreational vehicle) enthusiasts. While Las Vegas capitalizes on their flash, class, and nightlife, Laughlin represents itself as a "family-friendly destination." Since it is right on the river, outdoor activities like jet skiing and boating are a major focus.

Havasu National Wildlife Refuge

A great river in a dry, hot land attracts wildlife and people like a powerful magnet.
> —Havasu National Wildlife Refuge website

Just like the water, conservation legislation moved downhill from the Rockies to the desert. In 1915, President Woodrow Wilson signed the Rocky Mountain National Park Act, and twenty-six years later in 1941, President Franklin D. Roosevelt established the Havasu National Wildlife Refuge (originally named Havasu Lake National Wildlife Refuge.) The main reason for this action was to provide a habitat for migratory birds.

The refuge covers 37,515 acres near Lake Havasu, along the Colorado River in Arizona and California. The refuge includes more than three hundred miles of shoreline from Needles, California, to Lake Havasu City, Arizona, a distance of thirty miles. The twenty miles of that distance that flow through Topock Gorge is one of the last remaining natural (not channeled or rerouted by concrete) stretches on the lower Colorado River.

Being the largest river in the United States to cross so many deserts, the Colorado is naturally a major component of the Pacific Flyway. The flyway is one of four major north-south migratory bird flyways in America, and it runs the entire length of the Americas from Alaska to Patagonia (the sparsely populated region at the tip of South America). Thousands of migratory birds follow this route every year in the spring and fall, heading to breeding grounds, following food sources, or traveling to warmer climates to spend the winter. Havasu Refuge is within the Pacific Flyway, and more than 318 bird species stop there to rest and refuel during their long journey. This is also a prime breeding ground and wintering location.

Within the Havasu National Wildlife Refuge, south of Interstate 40, the Colorado River travels through Topock Gorge, a steep, craggy canyon hundreds of feet high and sixteen miles long. Northwest of there, Needles, California, was named for the pointy, narrow, needle-like vertical outcroppings in this canyon. At the end of the gorge, the river opens up into Lake Havasu.

Lake Havasu

The Colorado River provides water and electricity to an immense area of the West. Starting with Yuma in 1907, that region began to develop with the construction of large, strategically placed dams. From Flaming Gorge in Wyoming, to Glen Canyon, Parker, and Hoover dams, the river was harnessed, and lakes were created. Lake Havasu is one of those large reservoirs, this one created by the building of Parker Dam on the Arizona/California border, approximately 154 miles north of the U.S./ Mexico border, and 147 miles south of Hoover Dam. The 45-mile-long Lake Havasu serves as a storage area to hold Colorado River water, which is then pumped into two aqueducts.

The Colorado River forms the entirety of Arizona's western border, and the southern part of California's eastern border. It is the only squiggly border line on the map of Arizona. Although it is difficult to trace ancient desert people because of the terrain, archaeological records find evidence of hundreds of Patayan ("Old Ones" in the Yuman language) sites dating

back to AD 875. Among the Patayan's descendants are Mojave Indians. Because they live along the Colorado, the Mojave tribe's name comes from two Yuman words, "aha" (water) and "macav" (alongside).

There is some record of Spaniards in this area along the river, and in the early 1800s it was frequented by fur trappers. One of the first European-Americans to cross the Colorado River from Utah into Arizona was Jedediah Smith, who had also been with William Henry Ashley's Rocky Mountain Fur Company in 1822.

Lake Havasu City

Like Laughlin, Lake Havasu City is a newcomer to the Colorado River town category. Since most of the world's comfortably habitable regions were fought over, settled, and owned many centuries ago, the seemingly uninhabitable land was left to the dreamers to develop.

It wasn't until Parker Dam was built and Lake Havasu brought accessible water to the area in the 1940s that the land on this part of the Colorado River became a feasible place to live. But it was still many miles across the desert to the nearest city. Almost twenty years after the lake filled, there came a man, Robert McCulloch, who found just what he wanted there.

In 1958, McCulloch purchased 3,353 acres of property on the Arizona side of Lake Havasu. He continued planning for another four years, and

From country club mansions to truck campers, Lake Havasu City is a great place to spend the winter.

added 13,000 acres to his holdings during that time. McCulloch was born in Missouri in 1911. He graduated from Stanford University and built racing engines. However, his claim to fame was the development of the one-man, lightweight chainsaw. McCulloch bought the property on Lake Havasu to test motorboat engines. He also developed a retirement community on the shores of Lake Havasu. In September of 1963, the Mohave County Board of Supervisors accepted the establishment of Lake Havasu City.

London Bridge Has Come to Town, Come to Town . . .

Over in England in 1962, London Bridge was falling down. It was sinking into the Thames, mostly from the weight of traffic crossing over it. But this isn't the bridge that inspired the world-famous nursery rhyme, "London Bridge is Falling Down." Construction began on the "Old London Bridge" in 1176. Because the first records of the rhyme date from the 1600s, it was written about the Old Bridge. Then in 1831, the "New London Bridge," built several miles away, replaced the nursery rhyme one. When the second bridge was discovered to be sinking, it was put up for auction. McCulloch's bid of $2,460,000 won the 1968 City of London auction, and the bridge's outside granite blocks were numbered, shipped to Lake Havasu City. There they were reassembled in layers over a steel reinforced concrete core structure to make it strong enough for modern traffic.

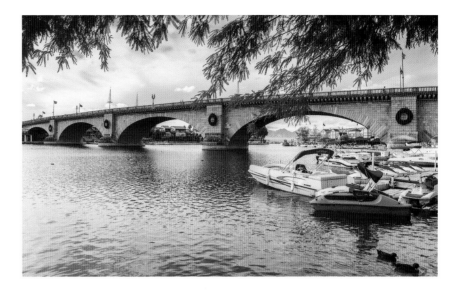

London Bridge has lots of shops, restaurants, and boat rental docks, a far cry from the majority of the river-bank experiences.

The Lord Mayor of London attended the dedication ceremony on October 10, 1971, and since then the bridge has fulfilled McCulloch's dream of bringing tourists to the city.

Bill Williams River National Wildlife Refuge

Traveling predominantly east to west instead of north to south as most rivers do in Arizona, the Bill Williams River is formed by runoff waters that feed into the Big Sandy and Santa Maria rivers in northwestern Arizona on the west end of the Grand Canyon. They meet and create the Bill Williams, which then joins the Colorado River at the south end of Lake Havasu. The land around that point, and all the way back up the Bill Williams River for several miles, was set aside in 1941 as the Bill Williams River National Wildlife Refuge.

Situated in a transition zone between the Mojave and Sonoran deserts, one can see saguaro cacti, stands of cattails, and cottonwood woodlands—vegetation that doesn't ordinarily live in the same region—all within one broad glance. The refuge hosts rare birds, such as the southwestern willow flycatcher and the Yuma rail, as well as neotropical migratory species. Other interesting birds found within the refuge boundaries are lazuli buntings, yellow-billed cuckoos, vermilion flycatchers, and western tanagers.

The Bill Williams River National Wildlife Refuge also hosts a wide variety of mammals, including desert bighorn sheep, North American beaver, gray fox, mule deer, ring-tailed cat, and collared peccary (javelina). Peccaries evolved from true pigs, not wild boars, and their presence has been traced to 33 million years ago in Europe, but not until 25 to 5 million years ago in the New World.

ABOVE~No matter what time of year, plant life abounds at the confluence of the Bill Williams and Colorado rivers.

RIGHT~The little lazuli bunting adds a splash of color to the muted desert regions.

Parker, Arizona

There were Mojave, Chemehuevi, and other Native American tribes living for centuries where Parker, Arizona, is now. The Colorado River Tribes Indian Reservation was created in 1865 for the Chemehuevi, Mojave, Navajo, and Hopi Indians. A post office was established in 1871, named for Ely Samuel Parker. He was a Seneca Indian who became an engineer, an attorney, and eventually a tribal diplomat. President Grant appointed him Commissioner of Indian Affairs in 1869, the first American Indian to hold that post.

The first settlement in the area was replaced with a second Parker, Arizona, in 1908, coincidently surveyed and laid out by Arizona & California Railway location engineer Earl H. Parker. The town of Parker was primarily a railroad town, steamboat and ferryboat landing, and farming community. Today, Parker, Arizona, is a river town, filled with retirees and water sport enthusiasts. Parker has waterskiing and jet skiing, vacation resorts, winter residences for RV campers, as well as many seasonal lodgings along the banks of the Colorado River.

The construction of the Parker Dam sixteen miles north of the town changed its character forever. In the 1920s, a group of thirteen cities formed the Metropolitan Water District of Southern California in order to obtain more water for their growing communities. It was certified by the California Legislature in 1928, and that led to federal acceptance of the Parker Dam project. The U.S. Bureau of Reclamation built the 320-foot-high (98 m) concrete dam between 1934 and 1938. The dam straddles the river between Arizona's Buckskin Mountains and California's Whipple Mountains.

From Parker on, the Colorado River is wide, flat, and relatively calm for the next 140 miles due south to Yuma, Arizona.

The Central Arizona Project

First proposed in 1946, the Central Arizona Project created one of the world's longest aqueducts, 336 miles (541 km), to raise Colorado River water up more than 2,000 feet with a series of pumps from the shores of Lake Havasu across the desert to Phoenix, and ultimately to Tucson.

Admiral Nellie Bush and the Arizona Navy

Water rights have always been extremely important in the arid west, and many Arizonans were willing to fight for their water. In 1934, as the Parker Dam project was getting underway, Arizona Governor B. B. Moeur called out the Arizona National Guard to stop construction. The water would have gone to southern California, but the Arizona Attorney General said that the Los Angeles Metropolitan Water District had not gotten permission to build in Arizona, much less take the water.

Moeur declared martial law, and sent ferryboat captain Nellie Mae Trent Bush, her husband Joe, and their two ferryboats loaded with twenty machine gunners and forty infantry to the California side of the river. The boats got snagged in some cable and had to be freed by the Californians. That was the end of the action.

Newspapers ran a picture of Nellie Bush at the helm of her ferryboat with the caption, "Admiral of the Arizona Navy." This appears to be the last time on record that one state took up arms against another in the annals of United States history.

Work on the dam continued while the U.S. Supreme Court adjudicated the issue and a compromise was reached. Arizona finally signed the Colorado River Compact in 1944, but battles over water rights continue in the federal courts to this day.

ABOVE LEFT~Parker, Arizona, is so popular with boaters and water skiers that one of the local radio stations is called "River Rat Radio."

As an indication of how serious and expensive water is for every western state, the project was not ratified by Congress until 1968, and not completed until 1994.

The Blythe Intaglios

South of Parker on the other side of the river, about fifteen miles north of Blythe, California, are some of the most interesting prehistoric pictures in the United States. They were discovered in 1932 by a pilot flying from Las Vegas, Nevada, to Blythe, California. Like the figures on the Nazca Desert in Peru, these figures can only be seen clearly from the air. The dry, isolated location accounts for their continued existence over many centuries.

Prehistoric artists created the intaglios (designs cut into or below a surface) by scraping away layers of pebbles and darker rocks to uncover the lighter soil beneath. While these pictographs made by removing gravel can be found all over the southeastern California deserts, the only ones depicting human figures are here along the Colorado River. Although it is difficult to ascribe a date for the intaglios, scientists have ascertained radiocarbon dates ranging from 900 BC to AD 1200.

According to Bureau of Land Management officials, there are three locations and a total of six clear figures, with a human figure at each location, and animal figures at two of the three sites. The largest geoglyph, a human figure, measures 171 feet from head to toe.

The human shadows at the bottom of the photograph give you perspective on the intaglio's size.

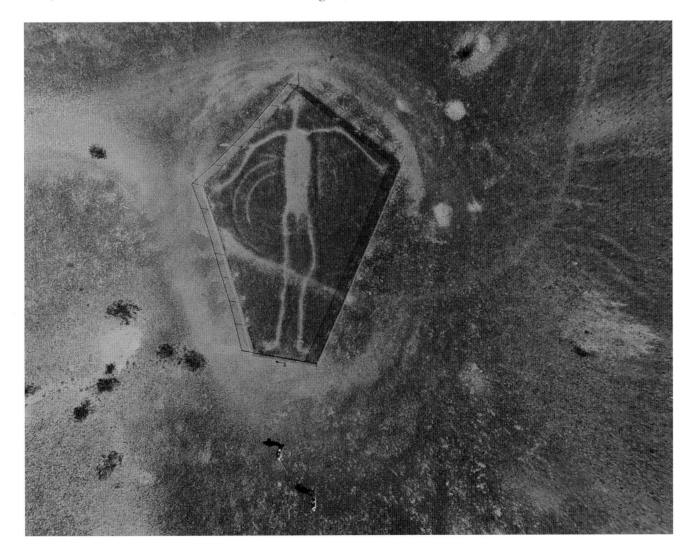

5

El Rio Colorado,
the International Finale

Spaniards on the Banks

Since humankind first learned to travel by boat, they sailed into bays, gulfs, and large river deltas faster and easier than was ever possible traveling overland by foot and horse. This was true of the Colorado, as well. Though the upper Green and Colorado rivers near their sources were first explored by fur trappers in the early 19th century, Spaniard Francisco Ulloa sailed three small vessels into the Gulf of California in 1539. He named it the Sea of Cortez after his benefactor, and conqueror of the Aztec empire, Hernán Cortés.

Jesuit missionary Father Eusebio Kino visited the Yuma area several times from 1699 to 1702, Juan Bautista de Anza passed through in 1774 and 1775 on his way to set up a Spanish colony in what is now San Francisco, and Father Francisco Garcés and several others were massacred by Quechan Indians at Yuma in 1781 while trying to set up a mission and a colony.

Steamboats on the River

It is a little strange to realize that the first mechanized transportation in Arizona, where about two-thirds of the state is desert, would be steamboats. But in the early winter of 1852, some Yuma Indians took one look at the strange craft on the Colorado River and ran away. These Yumas, also known as Quechans, had seen various boats on the river before, but never a paddle wheeler, with its smokestack belching smoke and sparks and its paddle wheel tossing the water into the air.

Starting with the 65-foot *Uncle Sam* in 1852 (the length of an RV towing a boat these days), various configurations of steamboats, side-wheelers, sternwheelers, and towing barges, sailed the Colorado until 1916, when several new dams made it impossible to pass.

The U.S. Army established Camp Yuma in 1850 to protect prospectors headed for the California goldfields. After much trial and error it was decided that a shallow-draft steamboat, one whose hull was so flat that it could float in less than two feet of water, was the only way to ship goods and people on the Colorado River.

But one of the strangest juxtapositions of transportation modes on the Colorado River came in 1858, when Lieutenant Edward Fitzgerald Beale

LEFT~A contemporary drawing of the U.S.S. Explorer steaming up the Colorado River.

BELOW~The flame skimmer is a medium-sized dragonfly prevalent on the desert stretches of the Colorado River.

arrived at the Mojave villages near where Laughlin, Nevada, would be a century later. Lieutenant Beale was ordered to build a road from Albuquerque, New Mexico, to Los Angeles, California, using twenty-five camels as pack animals. On January 23rd, 1858, Beale's camels were ferried across the Colorado the steamboat *General Jesup*.

According to Beale's reports, the camels worked well, but the commanding general of the U.S. Army was not going to have camels "in his army." Some of the camels were sold to circuses, and the expedition's lead camel driver, a Greco-Syrian nicknamed Hi Jolly, purchased several to use for prospecting in the Quartzsite area, not far from the Colorado River.

The Southern Pacific Railroad reached Yuma in 1877, and other rail lines reached Parker, Arizona, and various locations in Nevada in 1905. Gas-powered boats replaced steamboats, but the real end to boat transportation was the number of dams that were constructed on the Colorado starting in the early 1900s.

Dams, Canals, and Other River Controls

In the Yuma area, the problem with the Colorado River was the same as any other waterways in the Southwest; usually too little, but sometimes way too much, water. All the way along the river, the Colorado's natural cycle has been erosion and deposition. The river cut deep canyons for more than a thousand miles up to this point, and brought with it rich, fertile sediments to the valleys below. However, to create and maintain farms in the desert, the water supply had to be delivered evenly.

In the early 1900s, when settlements had just begun to grow around Yuma, the Colorado brought lots of water, but often in the form of violent floods.

Attempts to irrigate by canal, as had been done since prehistoric times, were thwarted by the radically changing water levels. All over the West, people were waiting for the water control that John Wesley Powell said would be necessary for settlement.

When Congress passed the Reclamation Act in 1902, political wheels turned quickly, and the U.S. Bureau of Reclamation began the Yuma

Two large granite outcroppings made this area, Yuma Crossing, the only feasible crossing point for the prehistoric Patayan tribes, the contemporary Quechans, and Francisco Vásquez de Coronado's subordinate, Hernando de Alarcón, who reached the area in 1540.

Project the very next year. The plan included the Laguna Diversion Dam, a pumping station for the water backed up behind it, and a series of canals to channel water, primarily for farming.

The location chosen for the Laguna Dam in 1902 was on a wide expanse of deep sediment wedged between mountains. Because only the ends of the dam could be anchored to the rocks, the engineers chose a different design, a weir. It backs up and maintains water at a certain level, but unlike a flood control dam where all the water is stopped and released in measured amounts, water flows freely over the top of a weir. The backed-up water forms a pool where water is channeled into a canal system.

The weir was only forty-three feet tall, with two-thirds of that below the riverbed. Thus the river was only raised ten feet. In spite of the many difficulties in obtaining rocks and getting the tons of concrete to the dam site, Laguna Dam was completed in 1907.

The Imperial Dam was constructed upstream in 1938 and the Laguna Dam's diversion outlets were closed in 1948. The success of Laguna Dam and the Yuma Project led to other Colorado River projects. Today there are five major dams on the Colorado River in the United States: Imperial, Parker, Davis, Hoover, and Glen Canyon, plus several smaller water diversions. Now that the water was under control, southern California and Arizona became the largest produce growers in the nation.

Eat Your Broccoli Thanks to the Colorado River

All that water made available by the Bureau of Reclamation projects, as well as state and local irrigation projects, created the nation's largest vegetable garden. With its rich soil, water, and sunshine almost every day of the year, Yuma County is the nation's third largest vegetable producer. It has the country's longest growing season, and produces 90 percent of the nation's leafy vegetables between November and March.

Dirt and water make all this possible. Like the River Nile in Egypt, by dumping silt in the Yuma Valley for thousands of years, the Colorado River created some of the world's most fertile soil. In 1928, geographical engineer J. O. Turle determined that the Colorado River Delta is one of the world's largest silt deposits. When Frank Waters wrote *The Colorado* in 1936, he estimated that "the river has gouged out of the Grand Canyon alone 350 cubic miles of rock," and deposited that at the mouth of the river. At the time, before several new dams were built south of Hoover Dam, Waters estimated that the river carried an average of "one million tons of sand, equivalent to 80,000 railroad carloads," through the Grand Canyon every day.

In 1914, the Bureau built the Yuma Siphon, a huge tunnel under the riverbed that delivers water to local irrigation systems. Near the border, the Colorado River takes on a whole new role—watering can to the largest agricultural area in California, Arizona, and northern Mexico.

The Mexicali Valley

The Cocopah hunted and fished in the Colorado River Delta, as probably did their prehistoric ancestors. In the 1850s, a Southern Pacific Railroad geologist discovered what indigenous peoples had known for centuries; that the thick Colorado River silt deposits near the gulf made excellent farmland. The silt extended west of the river, but the area was sparsely populated until the 1880s.

In 1888, the Mexican government granted a large part of northern Baja, California, to already wealthy landowner Guillermo Andrade in exchange for his support. Then in 1900, Mexican President Porfirio Díaz gave the California Development Company permission to dig a canal from the Colorado River to Mexico's Arroyo Alamo (a dry basin) and back across the border into southern California.

Developers gave the dry, desolate area along the U.S./Mexico border from the Colorado River to the Salton Sea, where "not a tree could be seen for one hundred miles," the pretentious name "Imperial Valley" to attract farmers to settle there. Five hundred farmers arrived by 1903, and by 1904 there were 10,000 people settled on the land, growing fruit, cotton, and vegetables on 100,000 acres of irrigated land. The combined names of the farming communities became Calexico on the U.S. side of the border and Mexicali on the Mexican side.

One of the largest and most fertile valleys in Mexico, the Mexicali Valley grows more than fifty different crops a year, primarily wheat, cotton, alfalfa, green onions, and asparagus, and its production rates are similar to those of the Imperial Valley in California.

Imperial Wildlife Refuge near Smoke Tree Point, about thirty miles northeast of Yuma, Arizona.

The Imperial Valley

Imperial County farmers grew 1,736,000 tons of hay for California's dairies in 2011, which accounted for 20 percent of the nation's dairy production. The valley is one of the state's top producers of spinach, potatoes, cauliflower, sweet corn, broccoli, and onions, providing two-thirds of the vegetables consumed nationally in the winter months every year. It is estimated that Imperial Valley farmers grew enough carrots in 2011 to serve a three-ounce serving to about two-thirds of the earth's population.

In addition, the Colorado River carries one ton of salt into the Valley with every acre-foot of water annually. Many of the areas the river passes through, especially the Tavaputs and Colorado plateaus, were once ocean floors; thus, the salt is contained in the rocks that the river erodes and carries away in its long journey. Farmers use subsurface drainage systems to remove the salt. Because of this huge amount of salt delivered to the Colorado River Delta, the nation's largest desalting plant is also located near Yuma.

Fresh water is important for humans and the crops they consume, but not all living things in this area need a large water supply to survive. The Kofa National Wildlife Refuge is a case in point.

Kofa National Wildlife Refuge

Kofa National Wildlife Refuge (shortened from the original King of Arizona mine) is a haven for desert bighorn sheep, and was created by Boy Scouts. They took an interest because Major Frederick Russell Burnham, a co-founder of the international scouting movement along with Lord Baden-Powell, noticed that there were only about 150 sheep left. When the Kofa National Wildlife Refuge opened in 1939, Burnham was there to give the dedication speech.

On the flat desert basin around Yuma, Arizona, elevation 138 feet above sea level, there are jagged volcanic-based mountains in mottled shades of maroon, purple, and mauve. Although the area appears as desolate as a Martian landscape, it is home to kangaroo rats, badgers, foxes, pocket mice, and ground squirrels. Many of their bodies have adapted to survive on less water, and they get most of their moisture from the plants they eat.

The Gila monster, largest land lizard native to the United States, can be found in the Kofa Refuge. Diamondback rattlesnakes, chuckwalla (also a large lizard), horned lizard (commonly called horned toad), and desert iguana also share space in the refuge.

The Kofa Mountains north of Yuma, Arizona, are rugged volcanic remnants of the Tertiary period, 66–25 million years ago.

Into Mexico and the River's End

On the map the Delta was bisected by the river, but in fact the river was nowhere and everywhere, for he could not decide which of a hundred green lagoons offered the most pleasant and least speedy path to the Gulf. So he traveled them all, and so did we.

—ALDO LEOPOLD, *Sand County Almanac*, 1949

For thousands and thousands of years, the Colorado River flowed more than 1,400 miles from high in the Rockies to the Gulf of California (also known as the Sea of Cortez), where its waters blended with the Pacific Ocean. All large rivers find their way from the mountains to sea level; or, as with the Green River, merge with another large river and continue the journey. Thirty miles below Yuma, the Colorado River runs east-west for a while and is the border between Arizona and Mexico. Then it runs south for another eighty miles to the Gulf. One early traveler said that at this point the river begins "winding through a maze of salty marshes, desert, mud geysers and dry lakes."

But a desert river, especially the largest one in the American West, is different than the others. For the past two decades, very little Colorado River water, if any, has flowed all the way into the Gulf. West of the Grand Canyon, Hoover Dam, then Parker Dam, Imperial Dam, the Central Arizona Project, and various other projects along the arid stretches, water has been siphoned off, leaving a lesser and lesser amount in the river by the time it reaches Mexico.

To address the issue, government representatives for the United States and Mexico created the treaty for the "Utilization of Waters of the Colo-

rado and Tijuana Rivers and of the Rio Grande," ratified by both countries in 1944. This treaty created a bi-national International Boundary and
Water Commission (IBWC) that regulates water entitlements, and Mexico
was assured 1.5 million acre-feet of Colorado River water per year.

To adhere to the treaty, the Morelos Dam was constructed near the
town of Los Algodones, Baja California (in Mexico). Although the eastern half of the dam is in Arizona, Mexico is in charge of dam mainte-
nance. The dam diverts the remainder of the Colorado River water into
canals that water croplands in the Mexicali Valley in Mexico. The dam
is governed jointly by the IBWC. But like any situations dealing with
water in the desert, the solution turned out to be not that simple.

Salt of the Earth, and of the River

Because it cuts through ancient ocean beds, the
Colorado River is naturally salty and it has been
carrying large amounts of salt to the Gulf of California for thousands of years. However, studies
find that about 50 percent of the salt that the river
carries past Hoover Dam is from human causes
such as irrigation return flows (runoff), reservoir
evaporation, and municipal and industrial uses.

By the early 1960s, a dramatic rise in the river's
salinity levels made the water that Mexico received
from the United States unsuitable for irrigation
or drinking. The IBWC then created "Minute
242," an addendum to the 1944 treaty designed to
solve the problem, setting salt limits for Mexico's
portion of the water. (In diplomatic terminology, a "minute" is similar to
a memorandum, where officials of more than one nation sign a written
statement of agreed-upon actions regarding the information contained in
the "minute.")

ABOVE~In the Upper Gulf and Colorado
Delta Biosphere Preserve established by
Mexico in 1974, the Colorado River wends
its way through the tidal flats near the
Gulf of California.

LEFT~While seasonal in other places, black
neck stilts live in the delta all year long.

Instant Oasis—Just Add Water

In 1977, a large drainage canal was created to divert agricultural runoff from the Wellton-Mohawk Irrigation District into a barren area in
Mexico ninety miles south of Yuma, Arizona and twenty-seven miles
north of the Gulf of California. The plan, to ameliorate complaints
about the high salinity in the Colorado River water being delivered to
Mexico beginning in the 1960s, turned out much better than anyone
could have imagined.

Before the water arrived, the area consisted of vast
stretches of cracked, dried mudflats layered with salt. There
was no water, no plants, and no sign of life whatsoever.
Soon, a shallow lake began to grow in the desert. Not
long after that, fish appeared, then bulrushes and cattails
began to grow, and the lake became an emerald-green maze
of marshy lagoons. Like a desert mirage, an oasis appeared.
The area, now called la Ciénega de Santa Clara (near the
town of El Doctor on Mexican Highway 40) grew to 7,000 acres
by 1988, and doubled that acreage in the next twelve years. It is
now the largest wetland in the Colorado River Delta, and home

Begun as a result of a diversion canal in 1977, the Ciénega de Santa Clara is now more than 15,000 acres, the largest wetlands in the Colorado River Delta.

to more than 280 species of birds, fish, and other aquatic life. It is estimated that 300,000 migratory birds spend their winters there. As miraculous as this may seem, however, it is only good news for plants and animals that thrive in salt water. The river's problems had yet to be solved, but more solutions continue to be applied.

The Desalination Plant

In 1992, the $250 million Yuma Desalting Plant was constructed by a coalition of state and federal agencies to help the United States meet its treaty obligations with Mexico to provide 1.5 million acre-feet of usable Colorado River water to Mexico. To this end, the Water Quality Improvement Center is one of six national centers, and the only one focused on inland brackish water.

The Improvement Center's goal, in addition to providing water to Mexico, is to demonstrate how desalination could be an answer to the water needs of Los Angeles, Las Vegas, and Phoenix. The 60-acre Yuma Desalting Plant was designed and constructed to clean 73 million gallons of brackish water per day from irrigation runoff. Because of hydrology problems, costs, and political impasses, the plant has only run a few months since then.

Pulsing Back to the Gulf

After years of planning and collaboration, between March 23 and May 18, 2014, several groups got together to create an artificial "pulse flow," a surge of water that mimics a big rainfall or snowmelt. Under these conditions, the flow of water increases for several days or weeks, and then the input goes back to normal. Through cooperation with the U.S./Mexico International Boundary and Water Commission, the U.S. Bureau of Reclamation, and the National Water Commission (CONAGUA) in Mexico, more than 105,000 acre-feet (approximately 34 billion gallons) of Colorado River water was released from the Morelos Dam at the U.S./Mexico border into the riverbed where water hasn't flowed regularly since 1960. The last time the Colorado River flowed into the Gulf was during the wet winter El Niño weather episode of 1997–1998.

Environmental experts say that releasing water this way helps keep rivers healthy by spreading native plant seeds and helping them grow. The seventy-five miles closest to the ocean are wet from a high water table or tides that sometimes creep upstream that far. But the first twenty-five miles of the riverbed from the Morelos Dam on down have been bone dry for several decades. The flows succeeded in creating new native habitats, and negotiations continue to provide additional water deliveries to the area.

Everything is alive, dynamic with constant change. Even the stones breathe; water is electric; the air is luminous with the memory of belching volcanoes.

—ALDO LEOPOLD, *Sand County Almanac*, 1949

Epilogue

Angry as one may be at what careless people have done and still do to a noble habitat, it is hard to be pessimistic about the West. This is the native home of hope. When it finally learns that cooperation, not rugged individuals, is the pattern that most characterizes and preserves it, then it will have achieved itself and outlived its origins. Then it has a chance to create a society to match its scenery.

—WALLACE STEGNER,
The Sound of Mountain Water:
The Changing American West

OPPOSITE~The Colorado River frozen over near Fisher Towers, east of Arches National Park, Utah.

Uninterrupted, it would take about two weeks for a melted snowflake to travel from Cache la Poudre Lake to the Mexicali Valley. It took more than 30,000 words to tell about that journey, and it would take an average reader about three hours to read this book from beginning to end.

All those things happen in time, in a line from beginning to end, just as a river seems to have a start and a finish. But the river is happening in all those places all the time. The person who lives by the river hears the water moving past all the time, yet he is always in the same place. And it's the same for all those river towns, and their piece of the river. But as Heraclitus said, "No man ever steps in the same river twice, for it's not the same river and he's not the same man."

Like the Colorado River, there is no ending to this story. Whether the water reaches the sea or a farmer's field, it evaporates, snows down again on the Wind River Mountains and on the Rockies, and here we go again.

Suggested Readings

Abbey, Edward (author), John Blaustein (photographer). *The Hidden Canyon: A River Journey*. Petaluma, CA: Cameron and Company, 2015 (first published 1999).

Blackstock, Alan. *A Green River Reader*. Salt Lake City: University of Utah Press, 2005.

Dellenbaugh, Frederick. *A Canyon Voyage: The Narrative of the Second Powell Expedition down the Green-Colorado River from Wyoming, and the Explorations on Land, in the Years 1871 and 1872*. Tucson: University of Arizona Press, 1984 (first published 1908).

Dellenbaugh, Frederick. *The Romance of the Colorado River, The Story of its Discovery in 1840, with an Account of the Later Explorations, and with Special Reference to the Voyages…through the Line of the Great Canyons*. Mineola, MN: Dover Publications, 1998 (first published in 1902).

Fedarko, Kevin. *The Emerald Mile: The Epic Story of the Fastest Ride in History Through the Heart of the Grand Canyon*. New York: Scribner, 2013.

Fleck, Richard F. *Colorado River Reader*. Salt Lake City: University of Utah Press, 2000.

Kolb, Ellsworth. *Through the Grand Canyon from Wyoming to Mexico*. Tucson: University of Arizona Press, 1990 (first published in 1914).

McBride, Peter (photographer), Jonathan Waterman (author). *The Colorado River: Flowing Through Conflict*. Englewood, CO: Westcliffe, 2010.

Powell, John Wesley. *The Exploration of the Colorado River and Its Canyons*. New York: Penguin Classics, 2003 (first published 1875).

Powell, John Wesley, editor. *Exploring the Colorado River: Firsthand Accounts by Powell and his Crew*. Edited by John Cooley. Mineola, MN: Dover Publications, 2004.

Stegner, Wallace. *Beyond the Hundredth Meridian: John Wesley Powell and the Second Opening of the West*. New York: Penguin, 1992.

Waters, Frank. *The Colorado*. Great Rivers of America Series. Boston: Rinehart and Company, 1946.

Suggested Websites

The Accidental Wetland in the Colorado Delta, by Sandra Postel
http://voices.nationalgeographic.com/2013/04/02/the-accidental-wetland-in-the-colorado-delta

Ciénega de Santa Clara
www.geo.arizona.edu/cienega

Imperial Valley Irrigation History
www.gchudleigh.com/barbarahistory.htm

The Lower Colorado River—Needles to Winterhaven, CA, Yuma to Topock AZ
www.socoloriver.com/index.html

Mountain Man—Indian—Canadian Fur Trade, essays by O. Ned Eddins
www.thefurtrapper.com/ashley.htm

Tusayan Ruins National Park brochure
www.nps.gov/grca/planyourvisit/upload/Tusayan.pdf

Utah History to Go
http://historytogo.utah.gov/utah_chapters/the_land/greenriver.html

Places of Interest

Arizona

CARL HAYDEN VISITOR CENTER AT GLEN CANYON DAM
Marble Canyon Airport, Marble Canyon, AZ 86036
(928) 608-6404 ~ www.nps.gov/glca/planyourvisit/visitorcenters.htm

DESERT VIEW WATCHTOWER
Twenty miles east of Grand Canyon Visitor Center on Desert View Drive (Highway 64)
www.nps.gov/grca/learn/photosmultimedia/colter_wt_photos.htm

EL TOVAR
1 Main Street, Grand Canyon Village, AZ 86023
(888) 297-2757 ~ http://www.grandcanyonlodges.com/lodging/el-tovar/

GRAND CANYON SKYWALK
5001 Diamond Bar Road, Peach Springs, AZ 86434
(888) 868-9378 ~ www.grandcanyonwest.com/skywalk.html

GRAND CANYON VISITOR CENTER
8 South Entrance Road, Grand Canyon, AZ 86023
(928) 638-7888 ~ www.nps.gov/grca/index.htm

GRAND FALLS OF THE LITTLE COLORADO
Water flows only in March and April
http://navajonationparks.org/htm/grandfalls.htm

JOHN WESLEY POWELL MUSEUM
6 North Lake Powell Boulevard, Page, AZ 86040
(928) 645-9496 ~ www.powellmuseum.org/

LEES FERRY/LONELY DELL
Forty-two miles from Page, AZ, via Highway 89 south and Highway 89A west.
www.nps.gov/glca/planyourvisit/lees-ferry.htm

LITTLE COLORADO RIVER GORGE OVERLOOK
Nine miles west of Cameron, AZ, on Desert View Drive (Highway 64)
(928) 679-2303
http://navajonationparks.org/htm/littlecolorado.htm

KOFA NATIONAL WILDLIFE REFUGE
Forty miles north of Yuma, AZ, on Highway 95
(928) 783-7861 ~ www.fws.gov/refuge/kofa

LAKE HAVASU MUSEUM OF HISTORY
320 London Bridge Road, Lake Havasu City, AZ 86403
(928) 854-4938 ~ www.havasumuseum.com

LAKE POWELL RESORTS & MARINAS
100 Lake Shore Drive, Page, AZ 86040
(928) 645-2433 ~ www.lakepowell.com

MARBLE CANYON LODGE
Highway 89A, Marble Canyon, AZ 86036
(928) 355-2225 ~ www.marblecanyoncompany.com

WAHWEAP MARINA, LAKE POWELL
Six miles from Page, AZ. Fuel, store, boat service

YUMA QUARTERMASTER STATE PARK
201 North 4th Avenue, Yuma, AZ 85364
(928) 783-0071 ~ http://azstateparks.com/Parks/YUQU

Colorado

ALPINE VISITOR CENTER
Trail Ridge Road (Highway 34)
Twenty-four miles northwest of Estes Park, CO
(970) 586-1206 ~ www.nps.gov/romo/alpine_visitor_center.htm

BLUEBIRD CAFÉ
730 Grand Avenue, Glenwood Springs, CO (970) 384-2024

COLORADO NATIONAL MONUMENT
1750 Rimrock Drive, Fruita, CO 81521
(970) 858-3617 ~ www.nps.gov/colm/index.htm

COLORADO SKI AND SNOWBOARD MUSEUM
231 S Frontage Road E, Vail, CO 81657
(970) 476-1876 ~ www.skimuseum.net

GLENWOOD SPRINGS WHITEWATER PARK
Interstate 70 exit 114, West Glenwood, CO
http://glenwoodwhitewaterpark.org

HOTEL COLORADO
526 Pine Street, Glenwood Springs, CO 81601
(800) 544-3998 ~ www.hotelcolorado.com

MASONVILLE MERCANTILE
9120 North County Road 27, Masonville, CO 80541
(970) 667-4058 ~ www.facebook.com/MasonvilleMercantile

ROCKY MOUNTAIN REPERTORY THEATRE
800 Grand Avenue, Grand Lake, CO 80447
(970) 627-3421 ~ www.rockymountainrep.com

Nevada

BOULDER CITY MUSEUM
305 Arizona Street, Boulder City, NV 89005
(702) 294-1988 ~ www.bcmha.org

HOOVER DAM TOUR
Nevada State Route 172, off Highway 93 north of Boulder City
(866) 730-9097 ~ www.usbr.gov/lc/hooverdam/service

LAKE MEAD NATIONAL RECREATION AREA
ALAN BIBLE VISITOR CENTER
10 Lakeshore Road, Boulder City, NV 89005
(702) 293-8990 ~ www.nps.gov/lake/index.htm

RIVERSIDE RESORT HOTEL AND CASINO
1650 South Casino Drive, Laughlin, NV 89029
(702) 298-2535 ~ www.riversideresort.com

New Mexico

BERG/ANIMAS NATIONAL RECREATION TRAIL
Near Farmington Electric Utility, 101 Browning Parkway, Farmington, NM 87401
(505) 599-1402 ~ www.americantrails.org/nationalrecreationtrails/trailNRT/Berg-Animas-Trail-New-Mexico.html

NAVAJO LAKE STATE PARK
36 Road 4110 #1, Navajo Dam, NM 87419 (505) 632-2278
www.emnrd.state.nm.us/SPD/navajolakestatepark.html

Utah

ARCHES NATIONAL PARK VISITOR CENTER
Arches Entrance Road, UT 84532
(435) 719-2299 ~ www.nps.gov/arch/index.htm

BETTY'S CAFÉ
416 West Main Street, Vernal, UT 84078
(435) 781-2728

CANYONLANDS NATIONAL PARK
Forty minutes northwest of Moab, UT
(435) 719-2100 ~ www.nps.gov/cany/index.htm

DANGLING ROPE MARINA, LAKE POWELL
Forty lake miles from Glen Canyon Dam. Fuel and gift shop.

DEAD HORSE POINT STATE PARK
Nine miles NW of Moab on U.S. Highway 191, then 23 miles SW on Utah 313
http://stateparks.utah.gov/parks/dead-horse

DINOSAUR NATIONAL MONUMENT
11625 East 1500 South, Jensen, UT 84035
(970) 374-3000 ~ www.nps.gov/dino/index.htm

FLAMING GORGE NATIONAL RECREATION AREA
5995 Flaming Gorge Dam, Dutch John, UT 84023
(435) 885-3135 ~ www.flaminggorgecountry.com

JOHN WESLEY POWELL RIVER MUSEUM
1765 East Main, Green River, UT 84525
(435) 564-3427 ~ http://johnwesleypowell.com

MOAB INFORMATION CENTER
25 East Center Street, Moab, UT 84532
(800) 635-6622 ~ www.discovermoab.com/visitorcenter.htm

Wyoming

LOG CABIN MOTEL
49 East Magnolia Street, Pinedale, WY 82941
(307) 367-4579

MUSEUM OF THE MOUNTAIN MAN
700 East Hennick, Pinedale, WY 82941
(307) 367-4101 ~ www.museumofthemountainman.com

ROCK RABBIT COFFEE SHOP
432 Pine Street, Pinedale, WY 82941
(307) 367-2485
www.facebook.com/pages/Rock-Rabbit/110075589049963

SEEDSKADEE NATIONAL WILDLIFE REFUGE
Seven miles north of Green River, WY on Highway 372
(307) 875-2187 ~ www.fws.gov/refuge/seedskadee

About the Author

WHEN JIM TURNER WAS TWO YEARS OLD, his parents uprooted the family and left their Connecticut colonial farmhouse, inhabited by eight generations of family ancestors, to seek a cure for little Jimmy's chronic asthma. Growing up in Tucson, Arizona, a geographical health exile in the northern Sonoran Desert, Turner has always understood the importance of water in the West.

A late bloomer, Turner received his masters in U.S. history from the University of Arizona in 1999 at the age of fifty. He began his belated career as historian for the Arizona Historical Society in 2001, where he co-authored *The Arizona Story*, a fourth grade Arizona history textbook. He retired in 2009 to write *Arizona: A Celebration of the Grand Canyon State*, which was published just before the Arizona Statehood Centennial in 2012. Turner's Arizona history articles and book reviews have appeared in *The Journal of Arizona History, Arizona Highways, True West Magazine, The Arizona Daily Star*, and various newsletters and other publications.

Turner began his public speaking career in 1996 with the University of Arizona Speakers Bureau. He gives monthly talks at several retirement communities, and has been a speaker for the Arizona Humanities since 2009. He likes to say that he "has been a speaker for twenty years, and was only boring for the first five."

Turner joined Rio Nuevo Publishers in 2009, where he co-authored *The Grand Canyon from Rim to River* and *Arizona: Scenic Wonders of the Grand Canyon State*, and edited the third edition of Fran Kosik's ever-popular *Native Roads: The Complete Motoring Guide to the Navajo and Hopi Nations*.